Beautiful Work

BEAUTIFUL WORK

A Meditation on Pain

SHARON CAMERON

Duke University Press   *Durham & London 2000*

© 2000 Duke University Press

Printed in the United States of America on acid-free paper ∞
Design by Mary Mendell
Typeset in Perpetua by B. Williams & Associates
Library of Congress Cataloging-in-Publication Data appear
on the last printed page of this book.

Preface

After a certain age you can no longer avoid the conclusion that the world is not as you thought it to be. This book tells the story of an initiation into a meditation practice. It is Anna's initiation. Anna wanted to investigate the world as she found it, outside of her expectations, but she didn't know how to proceed. That is the work. The story begins in the desert. What is this desert? It is a place where you see clearly, and seeing clearly is shocking. It's disorienting. What follows are three retreats, the first one within a monastic community, the other two at a practice center for lay persons. A retreat is where you take a look at objects closely and *practice* seeing them clearly, and where you try to recognize the difference between seeing and remembering. In the stillness there are voices: voices of the dead; voices that can't be identified; and the voices that can be. Anna listens to what they say so she can separate the voices that teach from the ones that torment. Also, she must discern what is essential for practice from what is merely formal. Renunciation is elegant, but is it a necessary condition? Can you practice and also love? The periods of formal practice occur over two years: they have beginnings and ends. But what of beginnings and ends that cannot be marked? Anna is astonished. Consolations diminish as she sees more precisely. This is not a hopeful practice. In the course of this practice Anna makes no pretense of gaining any knowledge, except about a direction that tends toward the truthful.

Beautiful Work begins in the desert, but it ends in the world. The world in which it ends, however, is not different from the desert. There are the same elements: what is seen, what is heard, what is tasted, what is touched, what is smelled, what is thought. Those *are* the elements.

I

Pain is original and pure. It is the first thing. Before language, before thought, and independent of circumstance. Pain is before injury. Arising from no fact, fortuitously.

To be competent to speak of pain is to speak of pain that isn't yours. This requires experiencing pain that is yours. Pain experienced *as if* it were your own.

I speak of the pain that has no cause. This is not to say there are no causes for pain. That would be absurd. But pain need have no cause.

I speak as much for my own sake as for yours. When I first made this discovery, it was like a smooth stone in my throat. Smooth, but unmistakable. Habit is a drug. Only when I speak do I become conscious again of the stone in my throat.

The stone is a mystery. It is great good to know of it. I also speak for that reason.

Of course I have come to see that the subject is larger

than pain. But pain is how the subject was initially focused for me. I had no choice about that.

It is difficult to remember: "Pain isn't mine." But from this everything follows.

It seems that it might be possible to recover a time, prior to the stories that get attached to the pain, when the pain simply *was*. Before it was dreaded and hated, there was a time in my life very far back when pain was innocent of association, when it was neutral, like sunlight or like breath.

Nonetheless, with discipline one can recover, for periods of time, that first state. That is the work.

But what would be the motive? Why would one endeavor to recover just that? Pain is tied up in explanations, veiled by stories about the pain, buried in this and that history. The motive is to extricate the uncompounded thing, free it of entanglement, for the sake of looking at it. If my pain came to be like that, there might be a way to see it.

The stories one tells about pain are deep, are profound ones. Nothing is more legible than these stories. But something is left out of them. If there were no stories, there might be a moment of innocence. A moment before the burden of stories, and the belief in their causes and consequences. There were moments when it was not accurate to say in relation to pain "because of this" or "leading to that." These were only moments. But they were lucid moments. In these moments everything is free.

I know now after what has happened that there is a way to see below ideas, to see without ideas, or (since that is impossible) to see the exact place where the ideas intrude.

To see like that: simply because pain *is* that way.

I began to hunger for storylessness. Before experience had wrapped itself up in accounts.

Moments of such seeing have authority. It is not my authority. It is like bearing witness. I could not say witness to what. There was gravity to this. I had to pay attention. There would be meaning or there would not be meaning. Meaning would not come in expected forms. It might not come at all. Meaning was outside of the task.

I began to hunger for storylessness. But outside of a story pain didn't look like my own. It was the *narrative* of pain that I recognized as mine. I did not recognize the *pain*.

Outside of the story, it made no sense to say pain was mine. Pain was a dense sequence of rapidly occurring sensations. But even to say "Pain was this" or "It was that," to say "was a sequence of sensations," begins another story.

The story is a great solace. I was addicted to the story. Why put it in the past tense? Am addicted to the story. For if this and this happens, then that and the other will.

But if pain were only this burning, this twisting or chill! Pain before injury. Pain without cause. This taste, that hardness, that glimmer of light. When I saw pain in this fashion, saw it unfeatured—I could not even say it was "pain" I was seeing.

What if the word too were wrong? If the word too were subsequent? *It is pain*, but sunlight was in it. Sunlight and breath. Other facts might also add their names to what I saw was original.

But how to do it? How to see pain uncompounded? It would be like tearing down a house.

I would have to start with the foundation in order to determine whether the house was dangerous to work on. Was the house out of plumb?

I would most certainly have to discover the sequence of the house's construction in order to *un*build it.

I would need to learn what kind of frame and what kind of foundation, whether a stone-built house or a frame house. How the house was connected to the foundation. If the house were stable on the foundation.

In which systems was there failure? If the girder were rotted out, I must first support the floor joists from the bottom and then take the girder out. If the corner post were rotted, I would have to jack up the wall to bring it back to level in order to dismantle the house. So long as the house was unsound I couldn't dismantle it safely.

But once the house was stable, I could get to work. I would shovel off the roof shingles. Then I'd rip off the sheathing with my claw hammer. Then the trim boards, the soffit, and the fascia. There might be crown moldings, cornice details I would remove in pieces. Only then could I separate the rafters from the roof ridge.

But now the walls at the gable end of the house would need temporary support. How to brace the walls while taking down the house? How to keep the standing walls from caving in on me? How not to be destroyed by this work?

I could not unbuild the house.

Instead I left the house. I was homeless. I lived in the open.

*

Dharma was in the heat. After the three-mile climb up rocks from the creek; before the steep descent to Thunder River, I came to a valley. I felt the dharma of the heat's relentlessness. By its relentlessness, I recognized the presence of a law.

Grasses were there. They grew five feet back from the trail and were deep, rich green, and long, bent over themselves. There was violence in the insistence of the grasses on growing *here*. They were not the color of the cactus, or of the rocks, or of the flowers. They were not withered by the heat. They seemed part of another landscape—not the desert.

The grasses seemed to signify: abundance that thrives in spite of the heat. But as I walked, I saw the grasses, the flowers, the Utah century plant, each was ruled differently. The dharma of the heat was indiscriminate: what was lush and what was not lush here throve simultaneously.

Violence was in the indiscriminateness. There—in the canyon—at the bottom of the world, there was no principle. The *blossoms* of the cactus were fragile. But the *stems* of the cactus were rude and twisted. The grasses grew marvelously, other plants died slowly after a struggle. If the dharma were indiscriminate, how could it be lawful? The answer was hidden.

Violence was in the provocation to look for the logic. It was in the passion to look. I was compelled to look. But no matter how much empty sky there was when I looked up, the meaning was still above.

It was not down here.

The effort to distinguish between up and down was immaterial. I had walked for hours to get to the bottom of the canyon. This valley within the larger canyon which I reached by climbing up was also far from the top. The walls of this side canyon still rose above me to a plateau I couldn't see, and beyond that farther walls rose higher yet, out of sight.

Where I walked it was open. The openness was part of the dharma I could not penetrate. There was nothing to indicate that this object rather than that one was significant. A person could go crazy not knowing where to look. The openness imposed an obligation. I had to look *at* objects and *past* them, simultaneously. *It was certain: no thing was an end.* Behind this cactus there was another. A rock that stopped my eye one moment became trivial the next. I was obliged to grow indifferent even to a sight I loved. I had to see that the place on which I thought my eyes could rest, they could not rest.

Where I walked it was trackless. If I looked down at the path, I saw only the piece of trail where I was: definite, but incomplete. If I looked ahead, I saw an entire landscape, but I was outside of it. Ahead, everything was visible—the trail across the valley on flat ground, the grasses, the century plants—but it lacked depth. All I could count on was the heat, which I couldn't see. If here was where I had to stop, the heat would grind me into the dust on which I walked. *The heat was beautiful: it had no outside.*

The dharma is a path, a way, something I am walking *in*. (It was not a surface: it contained me.) But I could not recognize this path or say even, "*This* is where I am." Or "Later on I will be *here*." I could not think! I was dizzy, and I let my eyes go out of focus. The heat had a sound like the *nada* sound. Like the hum of bees.

I met a man with a pack and a walking stick who had lost his friends three days before. I hadn't seen them.

That morning I saw a rattlesnake asleep beside a boulder. The heat—the dharma—seemed more dangerous than the snake.

A breeze rose out of the heat. It was not a breeze that died down and started again, but was constantly the same. It did not come across the valley from a direction. I was hopeful, until I saw the breeze was only a lesser degree of heat.

It was heat in a different form. So even the breeze that was a relief was not a relief.

I walked on a path that was well marked. I walked in an open space. But I saw only this: Everything here was unalterable, the cactus, the flowers, the breeze, the grasses. The man would find his friends, or he would not. I saw: if I followed the dharma, I would lose myself.

*

Stories divide the world: the good from the bad, the chaotic from the ordered. Stories are intelligible. But dharma is not a story. Dharma is law. Why, then, tell this story? I do the best I can.

There was a girl who died by fire in her bed. Christa had brown eyes, blond hair bunched to either side of her head, and a worried look. She wore a green skirt with straps. Her white cotton blouse with short, puffed sleeves was starched. Christa, and also her sister, both died by fire in their beds.

When I slept over at Christa's house, I slept where Christa's sister slept. But *I* didn't die.

My mother told me Christa died. I stood in the kitchen by the Glenwood range. I looked at the linoleum floor. I thought about it. I disagreed. "No," I said, "Christa *isn't* dead."

When my mother's water broke, I saw it. I thought: "My mother is dying." Blood spilled over the yellow vinyl chair where she sat. The blood was brilliant against the vinyl and the bright brass upholstery tacks. I stood up across from her and clapped my hands. I said: "That's amazing: look at that."

No place I can go will make a difference, will change the things that *require* change. I knew this definitively. Nothing would be more absolute than this discovery.

There was pain on my mother's face as she turned it to

the wall. While my father and my father's sister got a pot to catch the blood that streamed down the yellow chair, I had a chance to look. My mother's eyes were closed. I saw pain behind the lids and in the corners of the closed eyes. They thought my mother would bleed to death. They were happy. They were excited. They shouted orders to each other. My cousin's mother had died when my cousin was born.

In dharma Christa was always dead!

*

Each thing is ruled by one law, one dharma, but differently. And since I only see a piece of the law, I can't tell how it operates. If I got to Thunder River—as I did, and found my friends—what of the man who lost his friends? Nothing *appears* to follow. The conception of "following" is too small.

They told me: "The retreat is at a Chinese monastery. The monastery is in a former mental hospital." Two institutions—the monastery, the mental hospital—I have worked years to keep separate. The monastery in the mental hospital tests the efficacy of this long labor at distinction. At the City of Crystal Mind, where I went on retreat with Sister Dassanīya and Achan Sati, the monastery and the mental hospital were in fact in one place. We practiced meditation in a monastery that once was a mental hospital!

Master Hua was Chinese. We meditated for two weeks. Master Hua's monks and nuns practiced Ch'an, their form of meditation, a very long retreat, a retreat for life. A strict retreat: one meal a day, absolute obedience. And certain ascetic practices that seemed extreme: as penance, they burned lines into their flesh. I saw this on the foreheads of three nuns. I saw singed flesh along both inner forearms of a nun who came from Poland to practice meditation under Master Hua. Under Master Hua, monks and nuns sleep sitting up. The accomplished ones sleep on their feet —leaning against a wall—so if they die during their sleep they will end their lives in a posture of awareness. Master Hua showed me that I cannot see this with equanimity.

But awareness does not discriminate. It does not reflect what it likes better than what it does not like. Master Hua gives me grounds to watch consciousness operate impartially. But I see *preferences*. Preferences for what can be looked at and what cannot be looked at. I also see my attention going *toward* what *isn't* there and *away* from what *is* there. In dharma there is no liking and no not-liking, no agreement or nonagreement.

I put my broom down and get nearer to the stains. I cannot determine what they are. *Women* were in these rooms. If Master Hua burned these mattresses, I wouldn't have to clean them. I want to burn the mental hospital out of the monastery. I want to purify my heart in a place where there isn't evidence that purification is impossible.

What woman's blood? My mother's sister died, in labor, young because the doctor wouldn't operate. He didn't want to look at her blood. The doctor let her scream for three days. Then she died. But in my mother's case, five years after my mother's sister had been killed, the doctors determined they *could* cut into a body without scruple. My cousin was wastefully born.

Let's suppose it was not women in these rooms. Let's say it is semen on this mattress. In this room that I am cleaning, I see signs. I see evidence of sex, birth, and death. Whether it is a man who lay here, or a woman who lay here, or a man and a woman, it is still the same. They say to me: "Look at what is beyond birth and death."

Trese, my mother's dead sister's child, was wild. In the

backyard, among the long, uncut grasses, Trese was a galloping horse. Her hair was red. It was the color of her mother's hair. Trese's hair streamed behind her. Trese neighed. She neighed and threw her body against the ground. There was a wire fence around the yard. Trese flung her body against the fence like a horse that wasn't trained. Trese screamed like the wild horses she loved. Trese galloped. She tried to free herself from her mother's body. *She remembered her mother's body trying to free itself of her.*

In dharma, Christa's death and Trese's life are the same.

I want one neutral room, one room without a history.

*

I'm curious about the locks—whether they're on the inside or the outside of the doors. Some doors in this place have no latches on the inside. All the rooms have slits that can be peered through. There are restraints where there shouldn't be and openings where there shouldn't be. I thought: This is not a normal place. Nowhere in these buildings is there privacy. No privacy for the monks, the nuns, or for the insane.

There are no bars on the windows of the building where *we* live. There are locks on both sides of the doors. But *my* door has no latch on the inside. I am a connoisseur of such detail.

I have come to this place because I want to work with pain. I want to know what pain *is*. I want to know what *my* pain is.

When Christa died, and Trese's mother died, I saw: *there is no whole thing.*

I saw all birth is a tearing pain. There is Trese's mother's death. There is Trese's separation from her mother. There is injustice that Trese will always know her mother as the *loss* of her mother. My pain is of these glittering facts.

Birth separated Trese *from* her mother. Death separated Trese *and* her mother. My pain is at death and birth. A stain marks the place where life is broken out of life.

But *I* can't mark the place. I see: I can't assign pain to this or that part of the experience. I can attribute pain to Trese as the *cause* of her mother's death. But pain is also before and after her mother's death. Pain is also Trese's. I can attribute pain to Trese's *mother* as the cause of *Trese's* pain. But Trese's mother *died* in pain. There is Trese's *mother's* pain, and *Trese's* pain. I can't remove the pain of the body from birthing. I can't remove experience from the pain of the origin of the body.

There is Christa burning in her bed. It *is* Christa! Her eyes are surprised when smoke fills the room. Christa had a mole on her face, a birthmark on the left cheek. The whole body is a birthmark, a mark of being born.

And if the cause of pain is taken away, there is still pain. There is *no whole thing.*

Pain is also mere sensation. Pain is behind the eyes. Pain is earlier than seeing.

I thought: wholeness is *in my mind*, but not in the *world*. I came to the monastery to work with that pain.

*

In the bathtubs of the mental hospital there are temperature gauges. Instruments to regulate the body's heat. Machinery to cool the body down. Desire arises and passes away. Arises and passes away. Sr. Dassanīya and Achan Sati both talk of restraint.

In the morning Sr. Dassanīya asks: "Have you found that following desire makes you happy?"

Sr. Dassanīya is a Buddhist nun from France who was once a dancer. I look at her closed eyes. I see past them into darkness and beyond it. What might it mean to aspire to live *blamelessly*? In both worlds—in Paris as a dancer and here as a nun—her dancer's feet are sore beyond speaking of. Some days in the monastery Dassanīya's body is so weary that at each step there is not enough air. Her throat is parched, and dust dries her eyes. In the afternoon around four o'clock there are storms that blow snow into her face and sting her cheeks. Still, when she turns to look around her, she can't help seeing that the world is breathtakingly beautiful.

One day at the monastery Dassanīya, whose name in the sacred language means "beautiful," wound a silk scarf, dyed the saffron color of her robes, around her neck. It looked ravishing. What if she is faithful to the *idea* of no desire, and not *reconciled* to it? What if for twelve years she's lived the way her vows prescribe, without being reconciled?

"Birth and death are conditions born of desire." That evening Achan Sati instructs us in the great sutta that frees from pain. Desire gives birth to sorrow, lamentation, despair, and death. Wisdom can stop the cycle.

But, I thought, desire is endless.

Achan Sati chants. Next to him is Sr. Dassanīya. They face us. *She is elegant.* In my dreams she says: "*Now that the sense doors—the eye door, the ear door, the nose door, the taste door, the touch door, the mind door—are sewn tight with joy, my body is more peaceful. I have one honeydrop of joy in my throat. Let me tell you about it.*" Her French accent barely inflects the English. Her saffron robes are draped around her. Her head is shaved. Her face is the more beautiful for this. Her skin is luminous.

The great sutta is impassioned: Anytime there is contact with the ravishing world, there will be an impulse toward it or away from it. Wanting or *not* wanting. Wanting what is *not* there, and not wanting what *is* there. Desire and aversion. The sutta repeats the jeweled words: desire, aversion, neutrality. These words are at the center. Everything flows out of them:—

Light spills into the sky and flows from horizon to horizon. Time and space, earth and air, flow. The cries of the birds pierce the dark flow. Dassanīya wakes to the sound of birds. A bird's cry stirs her thought. Dassanīya touches her neck, her face, her shaven head. Her head is a form like other forms. Forms are *beautiful*. All shimmering, all dissolving into nothingness, all nothing. She rises and washes her face. Cold water runs through her fingers. Her hands now make an arc of her arms to cup the water. Light comes and goes on the water. This is a dance. She dresses, binding her body into the robes. Her touch upon her body comes and goes. But the order of the robes holds her. The day, now *a huge vessel*, falls and breaks open.

Light in the sky is a watery blue. The blue flows into Sr. Dassanīya's eyes. The blue dissolves there. Dassanīya practices the form of walking. What is *not* form is also nothing, glimmers and fades into nothingness. Sr. Dassanīya's mind is cool and gathered up to begin the walking. Walking is falling forward. But Dassanīya's falling is also rising. It is the pattern of coming and going: the ground, the weight, the lifting, moving, placing of her feet, the air around her legs, the robes against her knees, the dewy grass under her injured feet.

She is walking in the morning light along the path of dharma. She walks with clear knowing and without thought. Sensations come and go. The flash, the glimmer, the thirst, the bitter taste in her mouth all fall away. This perfect walking is gratitude for no gift to no giver. Her beauty makes the discipline mysterious.

Why should there be so much beauty for nothing, for no one?

Sr. Dassanīya rises and goes forth. It is as if her feet are without injury. Now whole. So much joy from abiding nowhere! She is homeless. She has no teacher. If she appeals to Achan Paññā, he says: "You are homeless." Homelessness is her teacher. She is shelterless. She takes refuge in awareness. She is nowhere. She begins again, goes forth again. Is it still homelessness if it is so beautiful? There is only this beginning again, which has never ceased.

In the meditation room, a nun sleeps. Sr. Dassanīya, absorbed in her own practice, does not wake her.

Dassanīya is collecting her attention for the morning chanting. The Buddha image could be a pile of sand or a heap of stones or dog shit. It would satisfy her as well. But the candles must be lit exactly so. Her lonely delight is in the surrender to the discipline of the form. She holds the stick of incense to the flame. In her room, on a cardboard altar, Sr. Dassanīya has placed a transparent stone. Her mind loves transparency. But if the stone were a piece of quartz, or a common rock, gray, irregular, unpleasing, or shit, she would all the same offer herself to the discipline of offering. A triumph of craftsmanship, a stone, a heap of sand—she is indifferent. She kneels, lowers her body to the ground, and bows.

Sr. Dassanīya makes her back long, leans forward and extends her hands as if she had something precious to give away to no one. The movement is exquisite. *Movement* is nothing too. Weight falls forward into bowing. Weight rests on Sr. Dassanīya's arms. She chants in Pali. The other nuns follow her. She has the purest voice. But voice is nothing. In her mind, the Pali, the French, the English come and go. The sounds are beautiful, like snow melting.

Achan Paññā named her "Dassanīya." He said: "You are not beautiful. You must discern what *is* beautiful." It isn't the shimmering of the mind. Or the shimmering the mind goes toward. Not the dawn sky. Or the brilliant sky at noon. Not the evening sky, cool and lidless. Out of fascina-

tion with this or that, beauty is *made*. But *un*made beauty is
in not choosing anything, is in no preference. Sr. Dassanīya
surrenders to the form of offering everything to the per-
fection of this unchosen moment. But this moment is not
as it should be. This unideal moment is not as it was, or will
be, or might have been. The constraint of this moment is
Sr. Dassanīya's monastery. When Sr. Dassanīya chants, the
beauty of her face pales and fades. Can something, in truth
austere, be so rich? Her solitary voice is empty.

The chanting arises. The chanting is over. The room is cool
and silent. But the mind is not silent. The nun sits on her
mat. Desire comes and goes. Breath comes and goes.
Arises and passes away. So delicate, made of nothing. Pain
in the mind arises, burns, turns cold, passes away. Nothing matters but attention. Her mind is still. Then her
mind is not still.

Now nothing is large enough to hold the light, the
sound, the thought, the pain, all arising and passing away,
all flashing and gleaming. *In awareness there is no abiding.*

The doctrine is gorgeous. Achan Sati turns it and turns it
in his discourse. Its facets glitter like a diamond's. What
appears is impermanent. What comes to mind arises and
passes away. Like melting and freezing, everything in the
world is passing away. All dazzling. All transient.

If this is seen, *nothing follows*. Feeling arises. But desire,
and therefore *birth, does not arise*. There is no *becoming*, no
compounding, no dwelling. No thing in which to reside.
No residing! *Nothing* arises. Nothing is the ultimate aspiration. *Gorgeous!*

Sr. Dassanīya loves discipline as a dancer loves discipline. Like the delicate neck of a clear glass bottle, her
voice is a pure conduit through which dharma flows into
the world.

I study Sr. Dassanīya, my text. The scarf is wound around the beautiful sutta.

I look at Dassanīya and feel my desire to be taught desireless joy by one who is indifferent to desire. But Dassanīya awakens desire. I love to look at Dassanīya's body —Dassanīya, the dancer, who once trained her body arduously every day. Sr. Dassanīya's posture when she walks is still perfectly deliberated, like a model's. Sometimes she exaggerates her steps. I have seen her pause in first position. But can she sit and walk deliberately without supreme consciousness of her body? I desire innocence. But innocence doesn't look like Sr. Dassanīya looks. My own looking isn't innocent.

I go back to the neutrality of the practice of the breath, and watch it come and go. The breath seems a *neutral* object.

I see the out-breath end, the in-breath begin. The breath is a coarse stream on my upper lip. Then breath opens up. Awareness, unpossessible consciousness, sharpens. Breath opens further. There is only empty space, immense and bright, with breathing inside it. Breath grows cool and wide, like the barest touch of the finest silk, falling and rising in another weather. On the inhalation, breath sensations brush against the inside of my nose. The streaming sensations thin out as they flow over my cheekbones. Breath bathes and cools the inside of my eyelids. The breath stream is dense and warm on my upper lip as it falls away. The fall of this breath is *shorter* than the rising. I watch it with astonishment.

No breath moment is like another. There is no story of breath. Breath is not continuous. Breath changes. But awareness does not change. How can that be?

Breath comes and goes, and falls deep into my body. Between my breasts there is tightness. Long and sharp, breath twists and bends. Breath comes and goes nonetheless. The twisting relents.

Breath is drawn upward into my head. But my head cannot contain the breath, and the breath flows through my head outward where I have never been.

It is not my breath. Nor is it another's. It is no one's breath. Nonetheless, I am being breathed.

My mind grows still. Breath is the faintest touch. Breath is nothing. Bliss comes. Now the breath is *not* neutral anymore.

I am experiencing something I do not understand.

The nun who embodies innocence and the nun who does not embody innocence are the same.

If I accepted indiscriminateness, I'd give up hope of love. I would experience love like dusk or sleep, impersonally. Love would be unintelligible.

Desire returns. Desire for the teacher. Desire to see what follows. Desire to have some place to go.

Desire for the teacher, the one who can explain. But the teacher cannot explain. The teacher knows how to live in peace without an explanation. The teacher knows how to watch the mind that cannot accept the absence of an explanation. Desire for the teacher to *be* like *this*. If the teacher knows how to observe the impatient mind—to observe the suffering of that mind with equanimity—perhaps I too could know.

Desire to see what follows. To know if the man found his friends, or if he did not find them. To know if they were discovered dead, to know *how* they died.

Desire to have some place to go. The monastery or the meditation retreat, where there is dharma different from that of the desert valley, dharma that is *compensatory*, like providence. Dharma is cool. There is water on my parched lips.

But my desire is for love. Not the kind that exhausts

itself. I have no image in my mind, no *knowledge* of *that* dharma.

The lover with his fierce, intense look burns himself up. He is not faithful to his love. He betrays it when it grows difficult.

Or he does *not* betray it. He stands inexhaustibly with love in his eyes. He forgets the difference between himself and the one he loves, and comes to love only himself. The one he loves disappears.

Or he holds his beloved to him like a mask. He cannot see love and death at the same time. *He cannot see.*

Or he *does* see and he is afraid. He cannot stand to see love and pain wound around each other like tangled vines. He cannot see that love and pain grow stronger simultaneously.

Consummatory love *does not take infinite care.*

It is not loyal to the truth, and to the pain that is in the truth. If it could be *lucid* as well as steadfast, it would be pure.

My desire is for dharma. But dharma is indiscriminate.

My desire is for love. But love does not take infinite care.

I must see what Dassanīya's eyes are looking at. "If it changes," Achan Paññā told Sr. Dassanīya, "it is not desirable." When I left her, she put her arms around me to say goodbye. She was not in her body, *but she was not absent from her body.* To have passion only for the dharma. How?

Desire is hope for a moment other than the one that's gone before, and for a moment other than *this* one. Sr. Dassanīya said: "It was a long time in my practice before I gave up hope. I thought hope had exhausted itself, but years later I would discover, no, I was still hoping." To *refrain* from hope.—This seems the most difficult.

*

Isaac said: "Pay attention. Sit with your back straight. Fold your legs. The ancients taught you must *acquire a seat.* You can't just flop down. That won't do. A seat from which you can see everything." Isaac scratched his neck. Now Isaac looked at me sideways as if he were taking my measure. He continued:

"At the beginning breath is all we notice, and we do return again and again to the breath to steady ourselves. But when the mind is supple, like mine, we enlarge the field of attention so that the object of meditation is anything at all as it comes into and passes out of awareness. Let breath be our example. But what is breath an example of? When you become aware of breathing, you won't see something you've seen before. Breath looks to be a recognizable process. I assure you that it is not.

"Is the breath long or short? Coarse or subtle? Is breath labored? You might ask: *What is breath's nature?* I'm telling you breath *has* no nature except *change.* The same with thought, feeling, hunger, pain, boredom, heat, consciousness itself."

I said, "What about pain? That's what *I'm* interested in."

Isaac said, "Pain is inevitable, but suffering is not. You must practice to see the difference."

"Tell me how."

Isaac looked up at me. He raised his eyebrows. Then he said, "Practice is like learning how to walk. I will tell you a story: A man carries a bowl of scalding oil on his head as he walks through the rooms of a huge palace. His only care is not to spill the oil. He must walk steadily until his only care is abiding calm. I'm going to teach you to do that."

For a moment I was afraid Isaac might wink at me. I wouldn't know what it meant if he winked at me. But he didn't wink.

He continued: "When the man's step becomes certain, when his practice becomes sure, he's free to turn his attention to the rooms he walks through. Inevitably he begins to notice where he is. Now that his attention is collected, he sees the whole, perilous life of the palace. He sees his individual peril in the great frame of dharma. At a glance he knows who is having an affair with whom. He sees the many schemes and intrigues, even when they're secret! Above all, he sees the peril to himself of the burden of the idea of self that he carries. *The man has all his life been in terrible danger.* But only now is the peril *visible*.

"There *is* a way out," Isaac continued, "But first you have to know that you're in danger. Not knowing is worse than death."

"Many things are worse than death," I said.

Isaac continued, "Imagine you have the capacity to know the truth. Delusion alone prevents you from knowing the truth. If out of mere fear you turn away from knowing—think how freedom is squandered!"

"All right," I said, "I want to learn."

"Is that so? Okay, all right," Isaac said. "Then bring your attention to the breath."

*

I watch my breath. It is the *back* of the eye that the breath opens up, the nerve cells there, reaching farther upward into the head. It is the *breath* pulled up and down along my body that is painful. It is the act of breathing itself that abrades the back of the eye and opens it up. I can't breathe without pain.

Now, in Pali, they are chanting the great sutta about desire. At first I can't separate desire and pain. My attention flees into desire—away from the breath and away from pain. But desire and pain have the same *story*, images strung together that lead the mind *on*.——Under the auspices of awareness, though, pain exhibits its discontinuous nature. Pain remains vitally present, even recurrent, but unattributable. It is uncompounded and free. Pain is seen to impose no story. Therefore it is not my story or anyone else's story.

I saw this when my grandmother tied my hands to the back of the crib and I lay calmly on my back, looking upward. It was not that I could not move. I *could* move, though I couldn't turn over. It was not that I felt the injustice of the punishment. Because I couldn't decide if it were or were not just. I lay in the room with the door locked. I remember that lock. There were no sounds in the house. I felt I had been left alone. I knew I had not been left alone. The blinds were drawn. There was nowhere to look but in front of me. The room was dark. I was not uncomfortable. I knew my hands would be untied before my mother came home. I wasn't worried. My hands were tied low down on the bars so I had no trouble moving my arms. It was like stretching.

Whether my eyes were closed or open, whether I turned my head or not, or focused my eyes, I couldn't move out of the range of the same pain.

Pain was behind my eyes. It wasn't anything in the room. It also wasn't anything in my mind. I had stopped thinking and imagining. There was pain nonetheless. The pain sensations were inseparable from *seeing*, whether I closed my eyes or kept them open.

When I tried to imagine—the light on, my mother home—I could *do* this. I didn't believe what I imagined. The pain, which I looked at for two hours, was more real. I had been tied up—restrained—specifically to see that anything except the pain was unbelievable. It was not pain *at* something—this must be stressed. There was nothing— no content—to explain what I was seeing.

They keep on chanting. It is no content that they speak of.

Restraint is for this: to see the difference between pain and suffering. Pain is inevitable, but suffering is not. Suffering arises when I fight the world's lawfulness, the dharma. When I desire things to arise differently from how they do arise, there is suffering. When I desire that things which arise not pass away, there is suffering.

The child saw pain. The child didn't think it should be some way *other* than it was. The child didn't imagine a world without pain. I had not yet developed *ideas*.

I saw only what was: the crib, the rope, the pain sensations behind my eyes that had nothing to do with the rope. They were more binding than the rope. When my grandmother removed the rope, pain sensations remained. Pain was fundamental. It was like breathing.

But growth was loss. I forgot that pain was natural. I grew indignant. I suffered trying to make pain go away. There was pain that could not disappear—the pain of the locked room—and there was suffering which could. I had forgotten the distinction.

They go on chanting.

My friend, Al, died of cancer three years ago. I hear him speaking through his lover's throat, even though he speaks in his own voice. His lover's love for him gives Al a voice. He is wearing his glasses. It is night. His lover put his glasses in his suit pocket in the coffin, in case they should be necessary. Al *had* a lover so when he died he could still speak. It is Al's voice I hear, but his speaking requires his lover's memory of *how* he speaks.

Al says: "Pay attention to the ground. The earth where I am buried is deep. Pay attention to the grasses. They grow where you don't expect them to. And," Al says, "it seems to me conceivable that others could be buried on this very spot. So it isn't for myself alone I speak."

*

The night of the full moon Achan Sati tells us we will sit and walk all night. On the day of the full moon and the day of the new moon—they did this. We will sit and walk until 3:30 in the morning. Then we will chant the morning puja and begin the next day.

A man raises his hand and asks: "Why? What is the point of an all-night sitting?" Achan Sati says: "Patient endurance." Sr. Dassanīya says: "Because it *isn't* reasonable."

I'm afraid of being unable to sleep, of making no end to consciousness. I am afraid of not having the freedom to put an end to consciousness. I am afraid of the morning light that will enter the room, pale, brownish, like light that has been stained. I know that there is nothing I am willing to do that will put an end to consciousness.

On the wall of one of the buildings someone has tacked up a picture of Achan Cha, an esteemed monk. Underneath, the caption reads: "If you become peaceful, accept it. If you do not become peaceful, accept that, too." I *cannot* accept it, because of the peacocks. Someone gave peacocks to the monastery fifteen years ago. I've counted six, but only one peahen. The peacocks hang around the buildings, displaying their feathers, sleeping, or turning in half-circles, discontent. The peacocks are reminders of the banality of wakefulness with no end. The peacocks are the image of sexual display without passion or direction. The peacocks are on everybody's mind. I never see two

together, so I don't know when I'm seeing the same one
twice.

When the peacocks cry, the wall of my mind seems
thin. My attention goes to the sound. I can't tell where it
begins. With the man three rows ahead who is restless?
With the one next to me who is inconsolable? I don't
know how far the effects extend inside or outside the
room. I think at last the sound drifts outward from *my*
mind to the peacock's throat, and ends in a cry.

*

Isaac gave me my first walking meditation instructions.
We were in an empty room. He walked slowly with exag-
gerated steps across the room. I thought of the word
"anomalous." Isaac, walking, looked weird.

Isaac said: "Choose a path. You can walk from wall to
wall. Or you can walk outside from one tree to another.
Once you choose your path, you must have a deliberated
relation to it. You must be aware of the process of walking
as you are aware of objects that arise and pass away in the
mind. Action must not be automatic."

I said: "You are asking me to see the unconscious body
becoming conscious."

Isaac continued: "Bring attention to the leg as it is
raised, then to the *movement* of the leg, then to sensations of
the foot when it is *placed*. Learn what walking is."

I have been warned of the danger of remaining *unconscious*. But I now see the danger of becoming *conscious*: I
feel the terror of learning.

I'm frightened of the idea of watching a process like
walking in which I can't intervene. I'm frightened of
merely watching passively. I'm frightened of being trapped
in awareness without being able to exercise my will.

I said: "To make walking conscious is a practice for making other automatic processes conscious. But why isn't what comes into consciousness then subject to the will?" Isaac doesn't answer. Isaac is not thinking. For Isaac, *thinking* is an automatic process.

I see myself that awareness *can* intervene in certain habitual processes—in the production of suffering, for instance. But awareness can't intervene in pain. That would be like abolishing or creating one of the elements.

I ask: "What is the point of this, Isaac?"

He says: "Identify with the purity of your own heart."

I don't understand him. I ask again: "Isaac, what's the point of this?"

Isaac looked at me. He said: "Observe the impatience of your mind. Your mind wants to get ahead of where it is. Let me put it to you," Isaac continued calmly. "There's no destination to speak of."

But this night *Sr. Dassanīya* gave the walking meditation instructions. And *she* said: "If you keep attention on your feet, *you can't be conceited.*"

*

When Emma, the sweet junior nun, came to the monastery, Achan Suddha was the senior monk in charge. She paid her respects to him and told him she had come to be a nun. He said, "Welcome to Heartbreak Hotel." Emma smiled.

*

I start the night with good intentions. I'll practice sitting meditation until my mind becomes unfocused. Then I'll practice walking meditation outside where the rain will keep me awake. But by eleven I'm tired. I don't see the point of this. I try to bring alertness to my irritation. But I want meaning. I dutifully consider once again Achan Sati's answer: "patient endurance" is the purpose of the all-night sitting. "Sati" means "wakefulness, mindfulness" in Pali. I am tired. The great sutta glitters. All is arising and passing away. If feeling ceases, then, naturally, desire will shimmer and pass away. But I don't see how to make desire cease. If the deathless is merely an antidote for unfulfilled desire— if I desire innocence for that reason—I don't want innocence. I say this. But desire that is fulfilled and desire that isn't are beginning and end of the same text.

The moon is full. The clouds are blowing across its face. I go outside to walk under the full moon. I don't want to hope. I don't even want to hope that practice will make pain disappear. Hope is a betrayal. Hope is a mistake about reality. Hope is the mind that is always elsewhere.

I bring attention clearly to my feet. Hope disappears. There is only the uneven pavement on which I walk and the cold night air at 11:30. The smell of the eucalyptus trees and honeysuckle is also here.

I hope for something better than attention to my feet. But there is more than hope: there is the night, the clouds, the cold, the smell of eucalyptus, and *seeing* itself.

I see that hope to perfect the self hangs around my neck like the corpse of a dead animal—whether I am walking in the cold or sitting in the meditation hall or sweeping the infirmary mattresses, or fighting exhaustion in my legs, or irritated, or pleased that I'm not irritated, there is hope. I hope for a perfected self and for a moment other than this one, *any* moment. But hope is a locked room. A *different* locked room from any I've been in before. Hope is a room whose door I always thought *was open*.

I'm cold. I go in and sit next to Emma on the grass mat. Emma is still.

All the pain of my being is now gathered in my chest. The child thought pain was behind the eyes. Or nowhere at all, not possible to situate. The child looked at pain judiciously. The *older* child thought pain was inconsolable, and desired justice. If I look *now*, I see only pain sensations that collect into a stabbing in the chest. The beating begins. The beating is in my throat, then around the heart again. The sensations move outward toward my skin. Now they are on the *outside* of my body, beating against my body, on the outside.

I open my eyes. I see Achan Sati sitting with a half smile on his face, and Sr. Dassanīya, beautiful, draped in the saffron robes. A saffron blanket is wrapped elegantly around her shoulders. Her neck is tilted slightly downward and her back is straight.

I close my eyes. The beating stops. I feel a pressure against the top left side of my head. The atmosphere against the left side of my head is pushing my head. The breath, too, is on the left side of my body. There are no breath sensations on the right side. My left nostril is numb. On the left side the rigid structure of my head is collapsing. I am watching, and my mind is tranquil.

*

It is three hours later. The spectral disk of the moon is visible just above the horizon. The sky is streaked. The sun is rising behind me. The peacocks are awake and screaming. I feel dirty. I make my way to the women's shower room on the first floor. Someone is in the shower. I undress. Margo is there too. I *hate* Margo.

What do I hate when I hate?

Margo has no distance from her pain or from her need. Margo is doomed. Margo draws no inference from practice. Last night Margo spoke. She said: "I feel like one of the mental patients. When I look at my mind I see no difference between myself and a mental patient." Margo doesn't understand the *use* of awareness. Margo doesn't see she must look at her pain, not be absorbed and devoured by it. Margo spoke to Sr. Dassanīya as if they were alone in the room. Margo doesn't understand the difference between being alone with another person and being in company. Margo spoke in the dark room as if nothing could harm her in the room. As if she were free from all ill will. Margo had a shawl around her body. Through the shawl I could see the shape of her body, her shoulders relaxed, her breasts vulnerable and soft. The shawl didn't conceal her body, but Margo didn't know the shawl didn't conceal her body. Margo could so easily be killed.

Margo is an unconscious supplicant.

Now here we are, Margo and I, two naked women facing each other. I see Margo's body. Margo does not see my body. Margo does not see.

I have been up all night sitting and walking, paying attention. *Now I am merely body*. Margo's unseeing stare makes me see my body.

This body, this shit body, this body not being seen, this reduction to the body, this disclosed but unseen body, this for-nothing body, this unintelligible body. Not even the body of death, not the sexual body either. This is not the body that walks, sits, breathes, or wakes with desire. This is hatred for the one to whom my body is unseen and thereby disclosed.

Margo understands none of this. *Margo does not see herself or me*. This is what *I* see when Margo doesn't see me.

Not being seen makes me *have* a for-nothing body, an excremental body, a self that is destroyed or that has never come into being. The body reduced so far might as well be dead. But death would be a relief. Death would end the terror of my standing here as if I were *not* standing here, invisible.

The one who does not see me wills that I not be. I am obliterated. My hatred is at being the one that is annihilated. My hatred is a will to be, in excess of anyone's capacity to *threaten* being and in excess of anyone's capacity to *will* my being. My hatred is a claim to be, against what wills my non-being.

If I am made not to be, I am in terror. The trees, the sky, the walls of the room are part of someone else's world. Color drains from the trees, the sky, the room. Everything pales. The world ceases to make sense. It becomes an unintelligible inscription in the language of a culture that, even before my very eyes, becomes illegible. The people in the world are not dimensional. My hands are thin and dry and not dimensional. My hands are like pressed flowers, pale, yellow. They grasp nothing. My world is inaudible. My mind is inaudible. I can't hear it.

This must be what the transmigration of a soul is like. The self coming and going huddled with pain and uncertainty, with no time to live as people do who do not know of this. I have lived beyond my own life. I have experienced my death *before* my death. Now I live on after my own death, still conscious. In this nowhere state, there is only terror at being endlessly annihilated. Why was I birthed in order to be destroyed *like this*? Why was I birthed in order to be given this death-in-life?

I would be real and alive if someone saw me.

Margo and I stand naked face to face. The mirrors are clouded.

This violent pull away from not being seen is what hatred is. The great sutta says: birth and death are conditions born out of desire. If eye-consciousness arises at the eye-door and mind-consciousness arises at the mind-door there is desire or aversion, or neutrality, toward the object of consciousness. If I *see myself not being seen*—see before the violence of hatred arises—before revulsion blackens my mind, no hatred arises, no hatred passes away. There is no birth of hatred. There is only not being seen.

The light paled in the room where the child was. Then there was no light. My mother did not come to turn on the light. Still my grandmother didn't come. There *was* terror. I pretended I didn't exist. I couldn't pretend long. I knew I *did* exist. There was no way out of suffering by this means.

No one sees me. I can't move my hands. I struggle but the rope binds my hands. I arch my back. I try to free myself. What if I can't control the functions of my body? What if *death* comes into the room before my mother comes into the room and finds me soiled? What if I suffocate from terror at having to look at death alone? What if death suffocates me, always impending but *never* coming?

I try to bite the ropes off. My teeth aren't strong enough. I think of my fingernails. My grandmother painted them. The thought of the red soothes me. I lie still again in the dark. The stillness soothes me.

On the other side of the room, to the right, is the locked door. The door is thick and stained deep brown. Next to the dull brass knob, the door is smooth. The plate in which the lock is set is blackened with grime and fingerprints. I imagine resting my whole weight on the knob so that the lock will snap. The lock *doesn't* snap. All the resistance in the world is in that lock.

I see that my grandmother is without authority. Also without knowledge. I am sorry for her. *She* has locked *herself* in a terrible place. I cannot tell how much time is going by. I grow calm. It no longer matters to me if I am inside the room or outside of it. I know I will be in here again and out of here too. I see there is little difference between one side of the door and the other. I want to tell my grandmother this.

At the edges of my body, the pain begins to burn. I think I can regulate the burning by opening and closing my eyes. But there is no longer any difference between my eyes open and my eyes closed. Crying starts. *I* am crying. The crying distracts me. Again, I am still. If I knew who was doing this to me, I could be free of it. But there is *no person behind it.*

On the other side of the door are many things. In this room there is only pain. But now I am *interested* in the pain.

The room is calm again. The pain sensations do not come from the ropes around my wrists. Pain is because of nothing *in* the room or *out* of the room. There is no victimage in it. It is directed at nothing in my mind or out of my mind. If my body were free of the ropes, I would still be *in* my body. I would still be in a *separate* body. I would still have a body that *is* seen or that is *not* seen. There would still be pain sensations behind my eyes.

Margo does not see this. I hate the death that comes to Margo in the dark room.

*

We sit. I hear the *nada* sound—the bees that are not bees—and I experience, through the breath, the *transparency* of Dassanīya. Though my eyes are closed, I feel an inclining toward goodness which rises in *her* heart and then drifts outward. This movement toward goodness, this intent (whatever it is), which suffuses the room, has nothing to do with me, *or* with Sr. Dassanīya. The origin isn't personal any more than the object is. Here there is no narrative and—stranger still—no relation. I simply sense her aspiration, when an inclining toward goodness—that itself becomes goodness—rises in her heart. It may be *manifest* through her face, her body, yet (my eyes are closed) it has nothing to do with her face, her body.

It comes down to hope again. Hope wants the ones who are chosen to be different from the ones that are not chosen. Hope wants the ones that are chosen to love me, to *prefer* me. Hope imagines I could become *like* the ones that are chosen. Hope wants the ones who are loved separated from the ones that are hated by decisive and public marks. It wants the monastery to be different from the desert, the dharma of love from the dharma of heat—the heat with its pervasiveness.

Dharma is a critique of hope.

*

The hot water out of control burns my thigh. I feel the shock of my body. The mechanism regulating the hot water of the shower has broken. The scalding heat adheres to my body, sinks in, and spreads. My body convulses against the burn. I try to shield the burn, by turning my back to the hot water. I burn myself again. I hold my arm against my eyes. My fighting is blind. I can't move away from the source of the burn. The source is everywhere. My instincts are chaotic. I can't regulate the source, or the burn. My arms flail at the mechanism. The scalding water keeps penetrating my flesh. The surface of the burn spreads. I can't get out of the way.

I get out of the stall and look up. I see Sr. Dassanīya sees my body in pain in a corner of the mirror. I see her seeing a fragmentary mirror image of my naked body.

Sr. Dassanīya is fully dressed. I have always seen her that way.

*

At the end of the retreat someone is driving Sr. Dassanīya and me back to the city. There Margo will care for her. Sr. Dassanīya is in the front seat. I am in the back with my feet on either side of the alms bowl.

I say: "The Korean monk who laughed was asked if he felt grief when his friend, the nun, died. He said: 'Don't be ridiculous. She was my friend for twenty years. I surely felt grief and now grief is over.' But Achan Suwatt heard the explanation and disagreed. He said: 'Maybe the monk felt grief because he was still thinking of the nun as *his* nun.' Which is right?" Dassanīya thinks for a moment and then she says, "Perhaps the monk was feeling *her* attachment to him."

I ask the question differently: "Does the arahant—the realized one—love without attachment, or does the arahant not love at all?" I lean forward against the seat because the window is open, and I can't hear well. Dassanīya looks down. She says: "Love isn't *only* a feeling." Or maybe she says: "Love isn't a *feeling*."

*

In the desert there is no water. You cannot think. But there is a breeze.

Al says: "The breeze will kill you. It is no matter. If there is a breeze you can say metta meditation. The meditation on lovingkindness. You can wish others well. *Wish Margo well.* Make the intent strong so *Margo feels joy*."

One Sunday Al's lover came into my mind. I said metta meditation for *him*. Two days later we were speaking to one another. He said he felt a shock of joy on Sunday at 11 A.M. The hour of my well-wishing.

"Say it like that," Al said. *"Say it with intent for Margo.* Don't expect miracles. Your eyes will narrow as you start to speak. The muscles in your gut will tighten. You may gag. Say it anyway. Say it, though you can't imagine a reason. When your mind wanders, bring it back to Margo's way of speaking. Focus on her Southern accent, which you hate. Keep the accent in mind and say metta meditation. *Do not sleep.* If you expect to feel generosity, you will be disappointed. *Care for what you hate.* Continue without expectation."

Al is dead. Al and Trese's mother, and Christa, and my grandfather are dead. Al is the only one of these who can speak. He speaks with the voice of his lover. Trese's mother is in pain. The doctor does not care for her. *Her* mother is not allowed into the labor room, although Trese's mother cries out for her until the nurses' mouths tighten. My grandfather, Louis, gave his body to science. My grandmother can no longer remember the arms of her lover. In her great old age she gets into her bed as if she never had a husband. She lies in the middle of the bed without memory of him, on *his* side of the bed. She can no longer feel his body against hers, although for sixty years they lay together. Christa is always too young.

But Al has authority. He wears a clean, pale blue shirt, and his hair is still blond. With the glasses his lover gave him, Al can see.

II

"Observe the mind. *Name what you observe.*

"You cannot be too watchful. Let awareness fasten on the breath. As the breath rises, note: 'rising.' As the breath falls, note: 'falling.' If thinking arises, note: 'thinking, thinking.' Watch thinking disappear. Objects come and go at each of the six sense doors: ear, eye, nose, tongue, body, mind. *Be Aware.* When you make a mental note, for instance, 'seeing, seeing,' observe the mental note brighten the mind. The mental note makes the mind clear. The mental note protects you. You cannot be absorbed into experience *if you know it.*

"When you stand up—and throughout the day—continue. Hold alertness steady, as if you carried a brimming bowl of oil on your head. Do not let attention drift away.

"As you rise from sitting meditation, note the intention to open your eyes. Focus on the direct experience of 'intending' and of 'opening.' In the background, let the mental note arise *unobtrusively*, only loud enough to *hear*.

"It might happen that awareness itself becomes the object of attention. *Observe this well.*"

The technique of mental noting was new to me.

In my room, surfaces drew me in. I lay on my bed facing the window. My room was bare except for the meditation cushion on the floor, also facing the window. There was a tall white cabinet, with a shiny plastic surface, where I put my clothes. The four books that I brought from home to this retreat were also in the cabinet along with a suitcase. Three of the books had glossy covers. The pictures on the covers were complex. Their colors hurt my eyes.

In the corner, next to the door, there was a small sink. Its white porcelain reflected too much light. The walls were painted linen-white. Through the blinds, opened but not drawn up, I saw the wintry green against the upper pane of pine trees which, one by one, led the eye to the forest. It was four o'clock in December. The daylight was almost finished.

I could sit and practice here alone or I could practice with the others. I lay on my bed. I noted: "Despair, despair."

In my dream Achan Suddha said: "Moods, perceptions, thoughts, the body, consciousness—these are things we practice through *not* with. *The journey is through these five barred windows. You won't find out anything in that prison except that you are in prison."*

Achan Suddha's voice came to me as if over a loudspeaker. He had no body to be seen. I was walking in terraced fields of millet. The millet had green stalks and monkey-fisted tops. Close by I heard water rushing. I knew the sound came from a river, but I could not see it. Below, water pounded against rocks. The water was green and transparent. Around me were purple butterflies. Their wings were edged in black. From the bushes hung hand-sized spiders.

Achan Suddha said: "Everything changes except the space. In this field there is space. Do you see it? *You must pay attention. It could be that a thousand years ago something else was here, a dwelling. For sure there was a dwelling here. The dwelling was in the space, as now millet is in it. The dwelling disappeared. The space remained. The millet will be harvested. You can see—even though you've never seen millet before—that it is ready to be reaped. Children will come with scythes to do it. With grand gestures they draw their blades through air and lay the millet out to dry. The rice, too, is ripe, although you do not see it. It is in the same field, at another time.*

"Wherever you stand, whether in this field or in that one, there is space around you. You must pay attention. One day in this field there will be a different dwelling. When five generations have lived and died there (I must tell you the roof of the house will burn, and, thinking to live somewhere more propitious, the last generation will move on) there will still be space.

"If you look closely out from inside the house that's not yet built you can see stars at night. The stars are an illusion. It is space you're looking at. Between you and the stars there's space. Also around the stars. Even before the roof burns, if you stand inside the house, you will see the roof is an illusion. Of course in one sense the roof is solid. The roof keeps out the wind at night. But if the wind should happen to break through the roof, or if, during the monsoon the water might, or if as I've told you, the fire will, see how fragile 'solid' is. And even now, after the first dwelling and before the last one (I speak only of the last one I can see. For, be assured, I'm not omniscient), what you can count on is the space. As you see, there's millet growing there."

I waited for the voice to finish. In my dream I could not see the edges of the field where I walked. Also there were no people close at hand. In the distance I could make out a figure walking. It could have been a person. It could have been an animal, or it could have been nothing. I watched my eyes harden when they focused.

*

The next day I told Isaac: "The word 'despair' is nothing. When I look closely there is no despair, but rather twisting, tightening, loosening pressure.... But this pressure which we call 'despair' is different from the pressure of knee pain or the pressure of breath. Isn't it important to distinguish whether pressure arises from despair or from knee pain or from breath?"

Isaac said: "Practice noting."

That night I turned over in my sleep. I felt my legs lying against each other as I turned from my back onto my belly. My body was composed of warm surfaces exerting pressure on each other or on the world. The blanket was around me, but it wasn't a blanket that was around me. I was wrapped in warmth. I felt the energy of turning. My thighs and knees were made of shimmering quicksilver. Turning, half asleep, I heard the mental note "streaming."

I dreamed again. Achan Suddha said: "Bring to mind a room. The one you're in will do. You call it your room. It is your room, for a time. And it's arranged a certain way. The books for instance are in the cabinet. The door of the cabinet is closed. But still you see the books. We say, 'The door to the cabinet' and 'The door to the room.' But there is no door to the cabinet and no door to the room. And no lock on any door. In truth, what's here is only space. Look at what your mind puts in the space to make it less strange."

I could not see Achan Suddha in my dream, but his voice was still coming over the loudspeaker. He said: "Frankly, you're ignorant. It's not my business. Also, it's nothing personal. Others are ignorant, too. But you purport to care. I only say this now because I've been summoned. I know you didn't call me. You're ignorant, and, I have to add, you have poor judgment." His voice faded away.

I heard in Thai or Hindi ordinations being performed. In Thai a monk announced that ninety-five monks were ready to be ordained. Each ordination would take forty-five minutes. They would perform the ordinations day and night until all were completed.

How could I blame them for speaking Thai? In the dream I was in Thailand. Or for performing ordinations: I was at a monastery. But the voices, over the loudspeaker, drone on night and day, in languages I do not understand! When I eat, when I try to sleep, when I practice walking meditation—I am aware in my dream only of the ordination platform outside. The platform had no walls or roof. It was only a hot concrete slab at the edge of a forest where ninety-five postulants each waited for his turn. Over the loudspeaker the monk's voice chanted holy words.

I crawled out onto the hot cement. I sat at the edge of the huge platform. Flies buzzed around my head. I had come out to watch the goings-on.

If these words were curses rather than incessant prayers, how could I tell? My lack of understanding was irreducible. When I screwed up my eyes against the bright sunlight to look closely at the novices' faces I saw through the glare of sun they also did not understand. I lay down on my back on the platform and closed my eyes. The hot cement baked my heels. I was in my body. This much I knew.

*

Isaac told me to keep a notebook where I was to write down how I used noting in my meditations. This way he could check on my attention. I was to write down: objects as they arose; how I noted them; what happened after I noted the objects. I was to bring my notebook to him every other day for a ten-minute interview, to read a representative meditation out loud. He would comment, in his fashion.

The first time I saw him after receiving the instructions, he told me to read from my notes. I read:

"At the beginning of the meditation, breath entered my body at the throat. But there was no throat."

He said: "Go on to another entry."

I read:

"I felt the sensation of breath and noted it as 'rising, falling' in my chest. The breath sensations faded. Then I noted a sensation of excitement first at the base of my spine. I noted that it rose upward to my neck bone. I noted the sensation as 'burning' and as 'crawling.' Sadness came and went. It was connected to pressure around my eyes, and to the energy crawling up my back."

Isaac interrupted and said impassively: "Another one." I read:

"The sensation of breath arose. It expanded. It filled my body up to the collarbone. It filled my head. Then breath spread outside my body. My body was floating in breath. I noted this as 'floating' and as 'fullness.'

"*Breath turned to light which shimmered.* I noted this as 'seeing.' Light expanded in concentric circles outward into the world. I noted this as 'widening.'

"Waves of bliss opened outward. I noted this as 'sweet' and as 'rhythmical.' I felt excitement and aching in my chest and throat. I noted these. Then there was no throat. Air and light were where throat walls had been. I noted this as 'space.'

"My heart stopped beating. And a *sensation* of 'beating' in the area of the heart arose. In the inside of the chest walls where my heart had been, I felt the emptiness of my body. I noted this as 'yearning.'

"I couldn't feel the front of my body. Breath became light where the front body surfaces had been.

"I grounded my attention in the touch points of the sitting bones which I could still feel and in my shoulder blades which I could also feel.

"The breath light moved to where my shoulder blades had been. There were no shoulder blades any more. I noted this as 'breath light.'

"Then I felt a contraction in my throat, as if I were being strangled. I noted this as 'knifed.'

"I knew I must lie down. I did. My body was present, but it floated in light. Fear came into my throat. I opened my eyes."

Isaac said: "That needs no interpretation. Read more." I read:

"The sensation of light arose behind my eyes. I watched the light contract and expand. Now there was only one eye at the center of my forehead. Light leaked out of it until there was no light left.

"Silence arose as vibration. I noted this as 'hearing.'

"The hearing was grainy. *The hearing had the same texture as the light*. It was of the same grainy black substance with small flecks of white in it. I noted this as 'hearing-seeing.'"

I looked up from my notebook and said:

"Sometimes there is content to the meditations. Doesn't the *content* ever matter."

"No," Isaac said.

I was insistent: "I have felt inconsolable in these meditations. Inconsolable at being expelled from innocence. When I stop formal practice, it will be like dying."

Isaac said: "Read on."

I read:

"I felt the sensation of silence in my left ear and noted 'sound.' Sound strengthened, *turning into* a *high-pitched white vibration*. I couldn't tell whether the vibration was inside my mind or across the room. I noted: 'Not knowing.'

"Then I felt moisture in my eyes. *It had the same grainy*

texture as the sound. The eyelid also vibrated. I noted this as 'blinking.' The tongue pressed against the roof of my mouth. It too had a grainy texture. Streaming sensations of the out-breath on my upper lip arose. They had the same undulating movement as the lid closing over my eye.

"The vibration in my ear shifted to two points on the crown of my head and bore down deep inside through the back of my eyes, into the throat, sinking to my chest where the heart had been.

"The vibration shifted back to my left ear, and moved from the ear to the outside of my eye. The vibration turned white. I didn't know how to note this. I noted it as '*hearing whiteness.*'

"Energy got strong through my thighs and lower back. I noted this as 'static' and as 'prickling.' Then as 'desire.' Between my thighs there was pure vibration.

"My breath grew fuller, rising now from underneath my whole body and enclosing my whole body. Gratitude arose inside the breath where body sensation had been.

"The gratitude grew sharp. It grew *intense.* The intensity was painful in the place where the lids of my eyes meet the eyes at the backmost point of their connection, out of sight.

"Breath turned to light and gratitude faded. The light sharpened and my body dissolved into waves of light (except for the fingertips whose hardness I could still feel). The intensity was excruciating, especially in the eyes. My eyes therefore must also have been outside the light.

"Then pain arose inside light—pain *not in the eyes alone, but also in the light.* Then breath and light were indistinguishable. Pain faded.

"Bliss started to come. I heard the words 'This is relentless.' I noted: 'thinking.'"

I looked up from my notebook at Isaac. He said: "It is not enough. Read on."

"Isaac, my whole face got light. I noted this again as 'shimmering.' Light spread into my body where the 'rising' and 'falling' of breathing was. I noted the movement downward as 'streaming.' *The sensations of breathing and of light spreading were the same.* I noted the convergence as 'rising light' and as 'breathing light.'

"The sensation of cold air where the throat walls *had been* slashed across my body horizontally. I noted this as 'mutilation.'

"Air entered my body through the small of my back. It was drawn upward. I noted this as 'rising.' Air also entered through a hole in the shoulder blade like a spear. I noted this as 'piercing.' Once more air entered through the small of my back. Then my whole body was rocked and warmed by expanding light waves. I noted this as 'radiating.'

"*The fixed, separable referents of my body are fading into each other.* One part has the characteristics of another part.

"Now there is light instead of body.

"I looked again and again. I looked a third time. I saw light instead of body. I saw light."

Isaac said: "That's enough for today."

I said: "Have you no comment?"

Isaac said, "Yes, in the last entry you read me, you mentioned 'the small of your back.' *That's a concept.*"

*

That night I dreamt I lay in a rice field next to the terraced field of millet. The rice was golden and ready to be harvested. I had woven the stems of rice around me like a blanket. I lay on my side with my knees drawn up. A crow flew into my face. It began to peck my eyes. I tried to close my eyes, but the lids were gone.

Then the landscape changed to a road. I had had an accident. It wasn't my fault. In the dream I remembered Achan Suddha's words: "You are ignorant, careless, and have poor judgment." Also, he added, "you have made poor living arrangements. Needless to say, you are at fault."

A man had been hurt in a car. In the collision my car was also hit, and I was hurt. True, my car showed no signs of damage, but it had been hit, and I was hurt nonetheless. Yet I was being patronized. No one was around, but I was being patronized. A voice said: "This is Diwaldi, a holiday where all creatures are sacrificed. *Look at the goat's head there. See, the bloody neck where the head was severed from the body? Why should it be otherwise for you?"*

*

Two days later, I read to Isaac:

"In my left eye, but also in my right, I saw arcs of darkness. Then circles of darkness turned into light. The arcs and circles faded and began again. I noted this as 'seeing' and as 'closing.'

"Energy began to creep up my back. It burned into my back as it climbed upward. I noted this as 'heat spreading.' When the breath fell, energy spiralled farther upward. Breath and energy moved in opposite directions. I didn't know how to note this.

"Energy rose into all but a slice of the top of my head."

I looked up at Isaac. I said: "I can watch sensations carefully. But I don't know how to remember them as a story. I can't locate them in time. I don't know how to write them down."

Isaac said: "The narrative is immaterial. Storytelling has no function except to free your mind from the burden of remembering."

I said, "If I pay attention, something continuous is unfolding in these meditations *in place of* the content and the story.

"Form is breaking down. Light and vibration are piercing and eroding it."

Isaac was silent. I looked back at my notebook and began to read:

"The tip of my nose began to pulse. My nose, along the bridge, grew numb. *The numbness was slowly peeling away*, like a bandage being removed, upward toward my eyes and forehead.

"Again, the surface of my nose pulsed. Again, numbness returned and was slowly peeled back toward my eyes. The numbness spread until there was no face."

I read from the next entry:

"It was still. I noted 'hearing' and 'sound.' The sound inside the stillness turned to vibration in my right ear. It surrounded my body. Sometimes it replaced body. I noted 'vibration' and 'heat' in my ear where the vibration had started.

"In my chest, I felt the pressure of cold rising *inside the vibration*. The pressure of warmth falling arose also in my chest. *Breath moved at different angles against the vibration.*

"There was swallowing inside the warmth. I noted: 'Moisture,' 'pressure,' 'hardness,' 'streaming.'

"Beating began also inside the vibration. The beating was violent. I noted 'grating,' 'twisting,' and 'aversion.' The beating moved to my throat, and then to my wrists and fingertips.

"The edges of my fingertips began to tingle. *The tingling turned to light and shimmered*."

I asked Isaac: "At what point does form start being something else? If I looked at my body at these moments, would I see form, or would I see vibration?"

Isaac said: "It would depend."

I said: "No matter how insubstantial the form is at the

moments I have described, I can always say 'in my wrist,' 'in my fingertips.' I can always *locate* sensations with reference to the body."

Isaac said: "Of course. The body-memory is strong; it will never disappear."

I asked: "The *memory* will never disappear?"

Isaac nodded.

I asked: "What shall I do when the body turns to mere energy?"

Isaac said: "Don't do anything."

He motioned me to read again. I read:

"Vibration began on the left side, between my ribs. It spread downward to my thighs. It enclosed the middle half of my body. *There was a formless rapidity of movement rather than form.* There was pulsing in my teeth. There was pulsing in my left ear. There was pulsing in my temple. Then light spread to my face. Light spread through my body inside the avalanche of downward movement.

"Light was dragged like a great stone across my face."

"I felt the breath rise from the soles of my feet upward through the dense flesh of my thighs into the space of my lungs and heart. I noted it as 'rawness' and 'grating.' The rising breath was cold and chilled my throat.

"Energy arose in my left ear. It was a pearly white passing into colorlessness, which moved rapidly through my head to my right ear.

"I felt the sensation of 'beating' and 'rocking' in my heart *replacing* the beating of my heart. This beating grew more intense than the beating of my heart.

"The vibration passed through and beyond my body. Then the area of the vibration was larger than the area of the head, like blades of long, rich green summer grasses drawn upward and concealing the face that wasn't there.

"The fast colorless movement widened. I tried to ground my attention in the hardness of my neck and shoulders. I tried to ground my attention.

"But when my attention moved to each of these places, the place dissolved. *No part remained 'body' when attention went to it.*"

I asked Isaac: "Is my body disappearing like this because the mind is seeing dissolution clearly?" He was silent.

*

I left the interview room and went to *my* room. I lay down on my bed. My skirt is wrapped around my calves. I free them, and stretch. For a moment, I rub the heel of my hand against my thigh purposefully. I stretch again. I like to feel the tension in my ankles when I flex my feet. I stretch my arms above my head, and clasp my hands. I see my body as if I am inside and outside at once. When I am inside it, my tallness is sweet as a summer's day. I run my fingers through my hair, and feel the shape of my head. My body is agreeable.

I unclasp my hands and hold them in front of me to the light, palms to the window. I stretch my fingers. My hands are my good feature. Also, they can grasp a cup, close around surfaces, put objects down, open, feel heat, cold, textures, give joy, give comfort. Hands are reliable. Hands have great intelligence.

I put my right hand to my throat. My skin is pale. Others' eyes linger on my face. They look at the skin—pale, but clear, with a faint tinge of color at the cheekbones, drawn outward. My features are ordinary. My eyes are untrusting and common. My mousy, longish hair is common.

I rest my fingers lightly on my cheek. I say to myself: "There, there." My tone is knowing and dispassionate. My

own hand on my own cheek, but it is as if another held me
in his gaze. My eyes soften. My face is at rest. I see myself,
both the one who sees and the one who is seen. Therefore
my eyes are peaceful.

This body has memories. I like to see my lover, Samuel,
when he looks into my eyes. I like to feel his hands brush
across my thighs. When desire spreads outward from my
breasts, there is a flush of warmth across my skin.

In the whole world no body is identical to this one.

But this unique body that *was* beautiful is *not* beautiful *any
more*. This common body that loves and desires and *knows
what solace is* is being destroyed. *This ordinary body is being
disintegrated.* This body that walks with poise, briskly—my
recognizable body, all dissolving, all made into nothingness, all nothing.

These hands are no longer hands that hold and give
comfort. My slender body, the body of a woman who
runs, is being destroyed by conscious walking. Practice is
taking this body away. The delicate throat I have, I do *not*
have. All the hollows that catch the light and gather shad-
ows are nothing. Light is the same as shadow. My neck is
being crushed by beating and twisting. There is no difference between my ordinary features and features of gross
deformity, no difference between deformity and beauty.
My pale skin is nothing. Pale or dark, this or that shade the
same. Luminous is nothing. My hands are shells. There is
no grasping. No *comfort* in grasping. Grasping what? What
is a summer's day? Desire that spreads in my breast, turns,
shimmers, gleams, hardens into hatred, then glitters back
to desire and then is nothing, desire and hatred the same,
nothing. The bed does not hold up my body. Nothing
holds up my body.

I have no substantial body to give me balance. There is
nothing to balance.

I put my hand to my cheek again. Out loud I say, "There, there." I am uncomforted. I turn my face to the wall. I hear the words of an ancient lament, such as the venerable elder of a prehistoric village says with dignity—the dutiful words, comfortless—over a corpse not possible to be comforted, at evening when the sun goes down, the hour of the dead. Then they lay the body on the pyre.

*

That night a voice said: "You have all your life demeaned your life by making a story of it."

I was lying in a field of glass, among splinters of glass. The glass was dazzling in the light of the newly risen sun. I thought the glass was beautiful—shards and splinters sparkled all around me. I lay on my back naked in the glass. I watched the glass glittering in the sunlight. "Try to get up," the voice said. "Believe me, you can't do it. You think that this is beautiful, and so it is, from a certain point of view. But if you try to stand, you'll cut yourself. If you try to move, you'll find you cannot do it. It is too painful.

"There is no story but the story of glass: the story of exclusions and omissions, the story of the narratable world you try to put together to make it intelligible. That is the only story you can tell. Or that others tell. It's not unique. Don't think it is. And even if it were, it's just a story.

"You've been lying here so long, you don't know where you are. The glass sparkles like diamonds, it is true. But if the glass were really precious, by now don't you think you'd know it?

"You cannot see it but your back is cut and bleeding. It can't be helped: you're lying on glass.

"If you were to get up quickly, determined to get away from here, you would have to endure horrible pain. You could, perhaps, do it.

"Or you could stay here and try to piece the glass together—
mend the story—this way and that way, as you have for years.
It won't go together. It's as it is: fragments, small needlelike
shards, and glittering splinters, beautiful, as I said, from a certain
point of view.

"By the way," the voice said, "what is your name?"

Lying on the glass I said: "I don't think my name is mine. I
don't have a name."

*

That morning I said to Isaac: "When I examine my body
closely, I see gross and subtle pain. When I am aware of
myself breathing, the breathing is excruciating."

I read: "This is how the pain of breathing is. Cold rising
stings the back of my throat and drives away the words.

"A picture arose of a sore from which a scab had just
been torn away. The sore was held under scalding water.
'Imagining, imagining,' I noted.

"Then I noted 'hardness' and 'moisture,' 'streaming' and
moisture disappearing into the 'dryness' of swallowing.

"There was dryness and pressure in my eyes too as the
lids touched my eyes over and over again in 'blinking' and
in 'grating.'"

I said, "It's just the ordinary pressure of the lids against
my eyes I speak of." I looked up at Isaac. "When I really notice any part of how my body works, it becomes unbear-
ably painful. The lids, for example, weigh against my eyes.

"The sensations become so rapid. I can't note them fast
enough."

"Good," Isaac said. "It's good you notice that."

"No form remained by which I could be identified. There
was only light.

"The light intensified. My body cracked. Only remnants
were left.

"Fear came. I noted it. I tried to ground attention on the sitting bones, where my body reposes on the earth. The sitting bones dissolved. There was nothing solid. Fear came again.

"Even the raw place where the cold of the in-breath hit the back of my throat—even there—was only the throbbing of the light.

"I noted 'knowing, knowing.'"

"As soon as I fastened my attention on any part of my body, it too dissolved. My eyes were shattered into little slivers, pieces of debris, dust and sand. The eyes were fragments of stone.

"*Only 'knowing' remained. 'Knowing' was solid.*"

Isaac said: "The phenomena you describe are empty. They're unimportant. What matters is your awareness as you watch them."

I said: "Once I see my body disappear like this, it's impossible to say 'I am *that!*'"

Isaac said: "Remember what you have said."

*

I lay again in the glass field. It was night. The stars were made of glass. When I looked up I saw them glittering in the sky, cold, hard stars outside of all constellations. The sky was the color of delphiniums. The sky was like an awning. Someone had lifted pieces of glass and placed them in the awning. They were too close. They pressed in on me. The sky was not the distance that it should have been. Behind the sky, there must have been another sky.

The voice said: "You're still here. You have no good sense. Look at the stars. Why don't you look at them?"

The stars were throbbing as if they were hurt eyes. The sky was scraped raw. I saw a falling star. A piece of glass fell into my chest and began to pulse. The night cold pressed into my flesh, where the glass had fallen. I placed my right hand around my left breast near the piece of glass. I felt the contours of the breast, then the contours of the piece of glass. I tried to caress the piece of glass, a little triangular piece of splintered glass with flecks of blue that I could see because of the full moon. "Here is comfort," I said. My fingers stroked the sharpness of the surface, multifaced the way a diamond is.

"You have no sense," the voice said. "This is not a real sky. It's only what is put here so that there will seem to be a horizon. There are those who need limits, and those who like similitude. You might be one of them. If so, look at the sky. The stars are made of glass, just as the field is.

"Nothing will touch you deeply here. Even the piece of glass sticking in your flesh below the left breast. Can you even feel it?"

"I don't know how to move," I said. "I don't know where to go. You said it would be difficult to move. How can you deride and also encourage me? I'm cold, naked, with no blanket in this field."

"Oh, I can't tell you where you'd go," the voice said. "Nor how you'd move. To move would require of you extraordinary effort, I have to say. You'd also need to walk on glass. Certainly you'd cut your feet. Then, too, it would be even colder in the other place."

The voice continued: "The sky here is not the sky. This much I know."

I turned my cheek so that it was lying against splinters of glass. I felt nothing. There was no sensation but a slight pressure underneath the eyes. Around me glass, blue-green, edged with white—like waves of a sea—glittered in the moonlight brilliantly.

*

"The light was too bright. Light bled into my ear, which began to throb. Hearing and seeing were too acute. I noted 'shining,' 'gleaming,' 'opening.' Light bored into my eye sockets, through the lids, seeping into my cheekbones. There was no place in me that was not light. Then light spread out around me and filled my whole world. Light gathered to an annihilating focus.

"*Pain was under the throbbing at the center of the light.*

"Pain arises from openness itself. It arises from the direct experience of light. There is no longer any body to shield me from it.

"I began to shiver. With my eyes still closed, I reached for a blanket. When I draped the blanket around my shoulders, the touch of the cotton felt unbearable. There was too much sensation. There was beating everywhere: in my eyes, in the corner of my mouth, in my breasts. The world had become shadowless. There was no body, not even my own, between awareness and the light."

Isaac sat in front of me. We were looking at one another. I had been reporting to him now every other day for weeks. He was a master of saying little, sometimes nothing. *I, with my untrusting eyes, trusted this.* He made no promises or claims. Isaac's eyes were clear, neither trusting nor untrusting. If someone were to try to harm Isaac, they would have difficulty. If, for instance, someone suddenly were to draw a knife, where would they put it? They could try to pierce his heart. But he *has* no heart. Nothing much inside, but space and air. Very little. Isaac knows when to answer questions and when not to answer questions. Isaac knows what he doesn't know. Isaac has no personality. I feel great tenderness for this. I trust *this*.

*

In the dream I tried to move from my apartment. But before I had a chance to say I wished to move, the landlord arrived. The landlord insisted: "You're here illegitimately. It's no use to argue."

I said: "I agree with you."

He said: "No use at all to argue. I have my rights, and I can make them plain. You have no right to be here."

I tried to interrupt, but he continued:

"There's nothing you can say that would make a difference."

We were in a large room without furniture. The floors had been polished. The scratches in the dark oak shone. On the low ceiling a fan turned slowly. In the empty room, the air was still.

He said:"There is something you could *do.You could fix up this barren place. This place is hopeless. Nothing will give the room charm. The polish, as you see, is useless. You could try to make a home here, a* temporary *home. In the walls, if you listen closely, you can hear an animal crying. On that sound your mind can rest. There is no way to save the animal. The truth is: it is trapped within the wall forever. It will die there, and when its flesh begins to rot, you'll know it. Until that moment it will be good company.*

"There are infinite ways to be in this room.You can stand as you do now.You can sit, or lie, or walk.

"Also, there is the matter of the window. Somewhere there is a window, but it's covered up by plasterboard. There's insulation between the window and the plasterboard, so you can't guess from the draft where its placement is. I won't tolerate destruction. But if you place your hands gently on the wall and feel inch by inch, you may find it. Don't be dismayed when you discover the spot where the animal is dying. The window could be in the floor. But then again, maybe it isn't.

"With the correct implement (there are none here) you might find the window. If you did discover it, you could look out. I'm not saying where the window leads. There is a view though. Quite a view.

"In beauty it is finished."

"What did you say?"I asked."What was the last thing you said?"

"I said: there is quite a view."

"That's not the last thing you said. That isn't it at all."

He said: "You must be hard of hearing."

"Perhaps you *could stay," I said. "You could lie next to me.We could take off all our clothes. I could learn to make love to you. Even if you didn't tell me where the window was. If you cried out while we were making love, there in the corner on the dark oak floor, cried out in pleasure, as I stroked your hip, and moved my*

hand along your thigh and upward—whatever you said, I
wouldn't listen."

The landlord said, "I would like to feel your pale face next to
mine, and your long, smooth legs. But even if we lay like that—
like brother and sister—or if we lay like lovers late into the night,
and up again before the birds, and at it, able to sense the light
streaming in that we could not see, it would do no good. My kisses
would distract you from the animal crying and from the window.
I myself would forget that there ever was a way out of this room.
I'm willing, though," he said, "I'm willing to be your lover. I would
put glass between your legs, blue and green glass. It wouldn't cut
you."

"Just tell me the thing you said before. Tell me again."

I saw desire in the landlord's eyes. He said: "I forget."

*

I read to Isaac:

"The sound of the nothing that is turned to numbness
in my head, especially around my temples, just above the
hairline. My temples began to pound. I noted this.

"Light materialized around my head, pressing against
my ears. Light hardened and the life of my head was
crushed.

"The sensation of *bending* arose around my ears. *Numbness was being bent back along the side of my ears.* I noted
'bending,' 'numbness,' 'throbbing.'

"My whole head was caved in. I could feel the weight of
the inexpressibly heavy particles of light, pressing against
my head.

"Then the energy drained away. The form returned. I
noted it. Compassion arose.

"The acute pain of breathing was less. *The more I was
willing to pay attention to the violence of the light, the less
painful breathing was.*"

Isaac asked: "For what was the compassion?"

"*For the violence. For the bending of light around my head.* The shape of my beautiful human head is being altered. There is physical damage. When I stand up from sitting meditation, my head is not a shape I recognize. I feel compassion for the one suffering the violence. Also for the one suffering the strangeness."

"For yourself?" Isaac asked.

"I wouldn't put it that way now," I answered without thinking.

I read:

"Desire arose, but not *for* anyone. It grew intense in the middle of the light.

"Desire moved upward and outward from the sexual center of my body to my heart.

"Light flooded where my throat had been. Light sifted downward and mingled itself with beautiful desire.

"*There are degrees of formlessness.* In this sitting, light and energy were *around* my body. They were *in* my body. At moments they *replaced* my body except for the parts that touched the earth. *Then the parts of the body touching the earth also disappeared.*

"When they disappeared, a voice spoke to me in sorrow: 'This is unavoidable,' it said."

Isaac said: "It may be there will come a time when there is no body and when even awareness that there is no body disappears."

I said: "It is happening in my dreams too. My dreams are like a plow turning up a field for the first time."

*

That night I lay on a huge mattress next to Isaac. The mattress was on the grass. It was cold. Snow was all around us. We were naked. Isaac lay with his eyes open. He looked as if he might be dead. He wasn't dead. Worms crawled inside the mattress raising their heads through the holes where the mattress stuffing had been sealed in. We lay on the bed. Isaac looked up at the sky. The moon was wrapped in a cloud like a piece of candy in cellophane. The ends of the cloud were twisted tight.

I said to Isaac: "Here we are together on a bed in a field of snow."

Isaac said: "I can't tell the difference anymore between a man and a woman." He took my hand. He said: "I don't desire you."

I said: "But you stroke my arm. And now your hand moves to my hair and strokes that too. Your fingers touch my neck."

Isaac said: "There is a bone in my chest that belongs to you."

"Nothing is deeper than desire," I said. "Soon the wind will come up and it will start to snow again."

Isaac said: "The bone is deeper. If you could look at my eyes, you would see through them."

"They are facing upward," I said. "How could I look? We are naked on this bed, and the snow starts soon."

"It doesn't matter," Isaac said. "The snow will cover our bodies as they are. Turn your palms upward so when the snow falls, you can gather it. It will drift into all the hollows. Into the crooks of my arms, between your breasts. It will fill the space between my face and shoulders. Around the delicate clavicles. On both sides of the nose. Soon the throat will be gone, and the space between the shoulders and the ears. It will make a bridge between the hip-bones. It will drift under the calves. In the whorls of your ears where the sea can be heard. It will fill the space between my legs and melt into my eyes," he said.

"And mine?" I asked, "Are you speaking of my body or yours?" But the wind was up and I thought he could not hear.

Then Isaac fell asleep and began to dream. I was in his dream. I knew this as I lay beside him. There was no story in his dream, only colors: aqua and other greens and blues. Wheat was in his dream. The wheat was blowing across my face. He put his hand up to the wheat. Light shone through it. I could see the veins of his hands, crossing each other like flung strands of wheat.

"Isaac," I said. He was dreaming and could not hear me.

"Isaac," I said anyway, "couldn't it be since we are here together, lying on this mattress in the grass with the snow around us, and since also I am in your dream—the dream of the wheat and the veins of the hand—that we might warm each other when the wind comes up, as it does now. I'm not saying it would prevent the snow from drifting, as you predicted it would. But we could lie nearer. Your arm could rest across me. What do you think?"

Isaac couldn't hear me. Isaac was dreaming.

Then in the dream of Isaac on the mattress dreaming, and of myself there too, desire arose. It was not for Isaac. I tried to make it be for Isaac. I tried to feel that if only he moved nearer, there would be contentment. The wheat would blow out of his dream across my face. I would see his veins when he held his hand up against the light. Or, looking at his hand, I would see the wheat itself. We would sleep a little together and forget. His thin body would turn toward me, and in his huge eyes no longer looking upward (and not closed either) there would be curiosity.

But the desire was not for Isaac. It was not for the snow (which I wasn't afraid of). It was not for the worms. It was not for the touch of anything or anybody. Not for the wind to die down. Not for the light to be brighter or to be less bright. It was not for the colors in his dream, not even the beautiful aqua. It was not for the snow to melt in my mouth, though I was thirsty. It was not desire to be asleep or to be awake. It was not even desire to find the bone, the exact place where there was no difference between his body and mine, the part that we would each feel identically when the flesh rotted, if we could still feel.

There was desire, but it was aspiration, a going forth from desire. I lay next to Isaac who was asleep and dreaming. The aspiration arose above the hipbones and across my breasts and spread upward until it reached my eyes. Now Isaac's dream distracted me. I wanted nothing I could see. I closed my eyes, but I could still see into Isaac's dream—the wheat, the veins, the promise of the snow.

The aspiration burned against my face. It burned away images. It burned my face from the inside out. It burned away words. Only

*the word "mercy" remained. Aspiration burned through the mercy.
The clouds blotted out the moon. Blackness deepened. It began to
snow.*

*

I woke in my room. The room with nothing in it was
white. I could see the stars through the blinds. I woke with
aspiration.

I was alone and wanted to be alone. I remembered the
dream of Isaac and the snow. I sit up. The room is still. The
door is closed. *This* door is not locked. I can open it. This
room is also silent.

I put my feet on the rug. I drop down to my knees. I like
to feel the rug beneath my knees. Soft, but with no "give"
to it. The floor will hold me. I want to run my hands along
the walls, to see if perhaps there is a hidden window. I *remember*: that happened in the dream of the hidden window
and the dying animal.

I felt it would be a while until sunrise. I was hungry to
know the exact time. Then the hunger faded.

I didn't want to know the time. I didn't want to know
the meaning of the dream I had just dreamed, or the
meaning of the other dream with the dying animal.

I would have liked to find the window, but I knew that
was no longer possible. I didn't wish to know whether I
would be tired in the morning or I would not be tired.
Whether it would rain or would not rain. I believed it
would rain. Sitting back on my heels on the floor it felt too
warm for snow.

I was cold sitting on the rug in my nightshirt. I lay on
the rug next to the bed with my eyes looking up. In this
dark before the dawn I saw there was nothing to be seen
ever. There was no end to movement. Or to desire. I wondered how long I could lie there, still.

I thought: I will die in this room or in some other

room. I will die ignorant, not knowing anything of the snow that Isaac spoke of, or that I saw with my own eyes. If in the dream Isaac had looked at me, I would still die ignorant. He said that if I looked into his eyes I could see through them. But I *couldn't* see through them. Not in the dream where we lay on the mattress. Not in the room where I report to him.

I lay on the rug without moving. It was still night. It might be a long time before the sun came up, with or without the rain. There was desire, pain really. It began in my thighs and moved up to my groin, higher. It throbbed as it moved. It was not desire. It was pain.

Then Trese's mother, who died in childbirth, said to me: "You don't think, honestly, the pain is for yourself alone, do you?" She had finished with childbirth. She was only a voice, but still beautiful, as in the pictures.

Trese's mother said: "It is important not to confuse desire with pain. Consider my example. I felt only pain moving inside me refusing to be born. How many days I labored, do you know this? My contractions yielded me nothing. I forgot about the child inside me. I forgot about the child's father.

"The pain whirred inside me like an unstoppable machine. The nurse came by with smelling salts. I turned my head toward the bottle. The smell was acrid, like ether or alcohol, like spring daffodils. It was February. The bottle, as she held it to my nose, smelled like tears.

"I looked into the nurse's eyes. I saw that she was tired. She held the bottle to my nose. But she looked past me. She was thinking in Russian. I grew interested. There was life outside this pain in her plans for the afternoon. There was also life outside her plans.

"I didn't wish to be like the doctor whose lips tightened when he looked at me. I didn't wish to be like the nurse who didn't look at me. I didn't wish to be like myself who forgot the child who would not be born from my body and the child's father."

Trese's mother said, "There may be something for you like what

*the nurse brought me in the bottle. If you look closely at broken
shells when the ocean washes them up along the sand at high tide,
you may find it. Or in the air of a cloudless February afternoon,
at three-thirty when there is no promise of spring. It might be in
your lover's eyes. Look at him carefully. You will see he is not looking at you, though his eyes are fastened on yours. It could be that
as you climb the hill, you cry, 'It is wonderful, wonderful,' and then
pause as you hear your words echo. You know when you reach the
top you will only have to go down again to look for another place
that will make you cry, 'wonderful, wonderful.' It occurs to you, you
might as well turn around and go down now. The aspiration, I'm
telling you, is the only thing that endures. Count on it. You must
nourish it as you would a child. Allow the aspiration that emerges
from your endless desire to be insatiable. Look for it also," she
added, "in the dull heat of an August morning when the fruit has
ripened, the lilies are dying, and the jasmine of the air is too
sweet. Sweetness has nothing to do with what you have wanted.*

*"Look serenely at your discontent. The discontent will fade, as
pain fades, if you don't resist too much. I myself, as you know, died
in pain. I couldn't expel the pain. Of course afterward there was
a child, but not for me."*

The voice faded. It was cold in the room where I lay on the
rug. I wanted to lie on my side, to place my head on my
arm and to stretch my arm toward the door. But I didn't
move.

Stars glittered through the blinds.

This was the law of night, which I did not know. There
was also a law of day, which I did not know.

There was no space between night and day, except the
one my mind put there, in the images of the dawn rising
pink behind the maple tree. Also, in the thought of the rain.

I knew *my* door was unlocked. I knew I could get up. I
felt the walls around me. Perhaps there was still an animal
trapped inside. If my hearing were acute I would know
how many days it had to live before it could no longer sur-

vive without water. The cabinet (in which the books were) was solid.

If there were no cabinet and there were no walls, night would come in.

I wondered what images rose behind the eyes of the old woman, my grandmother, lying in bed, speechless after her stroke, with her eyes dull and unseeing, but open nevertheless.

What did she see? She saw the death of her son that came out of the birth of her son. She saw the death of the mother that came out of the birth of the child. At the moment of her dying she saw the lifelong catastrophe of her own desire.

"What's the matter? What's the matter!" Achan Suddha said. His voice was irritated. It came over the loudspeaker, even though I was awake. "The walls are a convention, merely. So are the images. There is the image of the window with the blinds and the stars shining through. The cabinet is also an image. If you lie very still the images will wash over you like waves over a dead fish as they lap against the shore. When the images wash over you, you won't be drawn in by the surfaces. You will yourself become a surface reflecting everything. Nothing will be too bright. But you must lie very still," Achan Suddha said. "How many times do I have to tell you this!

"And when you die there will be a sky burial. Your body will be torn to pieces, small pieces, little bits, to accommodate the vultures that pick at your bones and eyes. If this is distasteful, there's no help for it. You can stay as you are, intact, lying there in the locked room."

On the floor, next to my bed, I slept. It was good to be on the floor where there was no place farther to fall. The rug under my cheek was like the skin of an animal. There was no animal. It was cold. I didn't reach for the blanket. I brought my knees up to my chest. I will die this day or I will die some other day.

I wanted to die dreamless, on the floor. I wished to forget the difference between day and night. I tried to say metta meditation, but my mind no longer formed words.

*

"My hands were resting on something—not *my* legs. Then they were resting on nothing. Then they weren't hands—just sensations of warmth and pulsing, of pressure and air. I noted 'fear.' I watched the sensations change. Then I opened my eyes and saw my legs."

I looked up from my notebook at Isaac. I said: "Do you understand that I am pitiless, heartless!"

Isaac said: "It is just pitilessness. If you watched it without ego or identification, you wouldn't suffer."

"I want innocence," I said. I began to cry.

Isaac said: "If you saw clearly, you would see innocence everywhere."

I read: "*My beautiful hands were hollowed out from underneath by cold.* Heat and pulsing and throbbing, and spreading of pulsing hovered above the cold. Pulsing became light.

"My hands were resting on something. It was not my legs. My hands disappeared. The cold was where my hands had been.

"*Energy hollowed out the inside of my body so there was only vibration*, the motion of life, strong in my left breast and my temple.

"When my hands disappeared, and then my legs, when the top of my body was hollowed out, I tried to ground attention in 'knowing.' I couldn't ground attention."

Another morning I read to Isaac: "My body is there, but it is *not* there. It is there, but it is not *mine*. It is there, but *hollowed out*. This is more excruciating than before, when the body only dissolved into light. I am required to witness over and over again my body actively being annihilated. I am not permitted to identify with it as the object of the violence. But I must sit inside it—sit in its center—vigilant."

"The sensation of cold arose *between* my hands and my arms. I could feel it move through the area *where the wrists had been*. My hands weren't there any more. My hands also weren't connected to my arms.

"I straightened my back. Cold arose and hollowed out the front of my body. The sensation of cold moved up and down hollowing out my belly, my breasts, my shoulders.

"Cold and pressure came and went where the torso meets the bottom half of my body near the small of the back. The two halves of body were separated by cold. Air flooded between the two halves. My throat was separated from my head. My head floated on cold.

"This was repellent to me. Pleasure in aversion arose. I thought: 'Aversion will protect me.'

"I opened my eyes and bowed."

A few days later I read: "Light arose. I do not see light spread through my body except when *there is also light in the room*.

"I watched the light streaming in circles.

"A sensation of my legs not being mine arose. Legs were there. They were not my legs.

"Then the experience of floating in energy arose. *Beating inside the floating* arose, in my heart, imperceptibly.

"Hearing arose *next to* the light.

"Hearing sharpened *next to* the light. *No body intervened between the hearing and the light*. I brought my attention to knowing. I wasn't certain *what* I was knowing.

"A voice said to me: 'Do—you—think—she—again—last—night—will—bring—me—here?' This made no sense. It mixed past and future. The voice was insistent. It repeated the question.

"I said to the voice: 'I can't answer questions like these. Who do you take me for?' The voice was patient. It repeated the question.

"I was in doubt about where the light came from; whose the voice was; what the voice was speaking about. I was certain about the energy. I was certain about the floating.

"In this meditation, in addition to what was happening, there was doubt about what was happening. Added to the experience of the world there is doubt about the world. There is absolutely a world and there is absolutely doubt about the world."

I looked up at Isaac. "Don't you see that I am suffering?"

It was another night. I lay on my bed. The light of the room was off. There was a crack of light coming from the hall under the door, behind my head. The back of my head was to the door. But I saw only the light from the stars through the long slats of the blinds.

I thought: "I must talk to Isaac. I must tell him more about the doubt."

I sat up. I turned on the light. I wrote him a note: long and urgent. I made my letters clear. When I was finished writing, I looked at the paper. Tears came to my eyes.

I thought, "I will send it." I thought, "I will not send it." My lips were dry.

I saw conflict ripen. It flowered in my mind.

"What do you want?" a voice asked.

"Only to be free of conflict."

The voice said: "Well, then."

The conflict fell apart like petals of a rose dropping

away from a mysterious center, pale yellow-pink petals, soft, with the slightest fragrance.

The lights overhead were on. My arm covered my eyes. I slept.

My grandmother's grandmother said: "You're lost. You know this, don't you? But I was lost before you. It is handed down, genera-tion after generation. It is your birthright, as it will be your grandmother's. You come before her. (Don't bother me with questions.)

"You won't know if she recognizes you, or if she recognizes any-one. On the off-chance that she does, be gentle.

"They will say, 'She's not uncomfortable.' Don't believe it. You see her trying to speak. She can't do it. What does it matter—an old woman, like I was, lying in your bed, in her bed. She's stub-born. She doesn't want to die. The doctors are irritated. The nurses are tired of turning her. Her heels are sore from lying on her back. How can they say she's not in pain!

"She's confused by the lights in the room. They are above her eyes and in her eyes.

"She wants to live. That's why she endures the feedings. When you feed her messily, and squash spills to the left of her mouth, she turns her head to the wall. She may not recognize you, but she knows this: She wants to live.

"But there will come a day when she sits up—they sit her up —dressed, hair combed, with lipstick and her favorite ring. Then she will want to die."

I asked, "Why do you tell me this?"

"Because," my grandmother's grandmother said, "you said, 'the conflict fell apart like the petals of a rose.' If you feel the least alarm at what I say, if you should care, as she does, for the food that's spilled, and at how many times a day they have to change her—If looking into her dull eyes, you wish to rouse her, to say, "It's me, it's me," meditate longer in the night. Meditate until the pity disappears. You can do nothing."

*

I read to Isaac:

"Light starts up in my face. Light spreads around my face until there is no face. Then light moves into my breasts. Light itself is stable. *Only the place it manifests is not the same.*

"All things are a *single* thing. It has many manifestations. I can't see them simultaneously. Today when the changes came, I saw through them something *unified*. I saw the emptiness of all manifestations.

"What I experience as light or heat, as beating or as desire—is *one indivisible phenomenon*. If I could see clearly as I did today, I could never doubt this."

Isaac nodded. Isaac seemed absent.

I lay on my belly on the field of glass. I had turned over. My hands were cut. I could no longer see the sky. I was cold. Slivers of glass glistened like sand. I wanted to get up. "Can't someone help?" I asked. There was silence.

I heard the sound of a bird, but no human sound. The bird was far away. Also far away someone lit a lamp.

Achan Suddha said: "Unwillingness too is a mind-state."

I said: "I didn't call you. You're not Isaac. You're not the other one. Why do you talk that way?"

Achan Suddha said: "Notice your preference for openness and your aversion to it. Of itself, openness is neutral."

I said: "I didn't ask you anything."

"Sooner or later," Achan Suddha said, "judgment fades. The chance for judgment fades."

"You're not talking on the loudspeaker any more."

Achan Suddha said: "Either you can hear me or you can't hear me. Soon I won't speak at all. I'll be silent."

I said: "But the dead can speak. Al can speak. The dead can always speak, if there is a lover."

Achan Suddha said: "You can't verify what they say. Anyway, their words don't count."

"What does count then?" I said. I had stood up.

"The leaves do," he said. "You can hear them rustling in the night—the dead ones, if you walk farther than you have walked. The wind blows through them, curled against themselves and against each other. In the spring, if you walk farther, you can break a leaf from the branch, and feel the sap bleed through the veins. Rub the sap against your cheek. Keep walking. If rain should come, you will feel the wet of the night driving into your face...." His voice broke off.

"This morning for three hours I didn't move. I watched space. There were no objects in the space. There was space. There was knowing of space.

"Great desire arose under the space, first in my chest, then in my throat. Great desire has no object.

"Gratitude arose. It had no object. It too lay in the space."

For two weeks I didn't leave my room except once a day to go upstairs for a plate of food. I didn't write in my notebook. I didn't report to Isaac. I had no dreams. I saw no one. I sat and walked and slept.

On the fifteenth day I fell asleep and dreamt of the field of glass. The field was beautiful but empty. No one lay in its midst. Wind came and blew the slivers of glass away.

I opened my eyes. Sun was shining through the blinds of my white room. Ice hung from the tiny branches of two peach trees that lay between the window and the forest. Glittering ice crusted the branches. The door was not locked. Upstairs there were people. Isaac, for instance, was upstairs. I loved Isaac, pure in his intentions, whom I did not know. The sunlight was astonishing, burning. Ice melted on the branches of the peach trees. If I could lie here long enough, I would see grass and dahlias, new leaves on the trees, the birds nesting, fallow deer come to the edge of the forest. Then the snows would come again and again. The wind would break the branches of the trees. Flowers would bloom over and over again (dahlias and bluet), and grass would grow green and wither. Now ice was on the branches of the peach trees, melting.

A voice said: "Visions are insignificant. Today it is bright, but not beyond the ordinary—the simple light of day."

The voice said: "You'll have to leave this room, as you left the field of glass. The exact moment you grow comfortable, you must go. Don't look for the ones who've spoken to you. If you look into the space from which the voices came, you are looking past them.

"It may be you will spend your lifetime in a room like this one. I can't tell. It may be you are done with rooms."

The voice said: "Look at her. Her hearing's gone. She can't move. She keeps a gold chain around her neck out of vanity. When they try to take it off, she shakes her head, 'No.' She thinks she is her own child. She sees Louis, her dead husband. She thinks Louis is her father. Everyone she loved is standing around her bedside: the daughter, Esther, who's alive, Trese's mother, who is dead, Bill, her daughter's husband, and Rachel, her dead second cousin, the two great-grandchildren, of course, Ura, her companion, and Sol her dead son. She can't hear the living. She can't hear the dead. She can't hear me either. Look at her eyes!"

The same voice said: "She sees exactly what you do."

III

Then the voice said: "Why are you equipped to talk of pain? What makes you think you can do it?"

I said: "Who will talk of pain? Who is more equipped? I know now of the seed buried for years—the pain-seed, the one planted and covered with stony dirt so it would never grow. But it grew and flourished. At first it flowered like leaves of squash, big elaborate leaves with silver veins. One night I went out to the garden, late, and pulled the pain-plant out of the earth. It was a bitter task to uproot something thriving. I dug up the pain-seed too and all the roots and leaves, and made a huge pile of the debris. I held the fruit against my face. The skin of the fruit was delicate. The smooth green skin glistened against my cheek. Then I hacked the fruit to pieces. The fruit was milky on the inside—cool. I bathed my face in the juice of the pain-fruit."

"Get to the point," the voice said impatiently. "I don't have all day to listen."

"I buried the seed again in the stony soil. At night I went into *the garden late, after even the mockingbirds had stopped. I checked for signs of growth. I was scrupulous. Every night I pulled up tiny roots. Then my grandmother died. The pain-seed bloomed."*

I woke in my room at N———. It was spring. I came to this place to work with pain. But pain was too small to name what I saw. Pain was only one name. Inside of pain is the whole world.

I see the hard, round, whole substance of pain splinter and crack into everything there is. Light too is discontinuous and impersonal. And so is the self discontinuous and impersonal. The shattering runs through everything. Joy is one mind-moment that flickers and falls apart. Awareness is one mind-moment, then another mind-moment, then another one. Between mind-moments, nothing. When awareness is smooth, like a glassy lake, I see the nothing. Then it isn't pain I'm looking at. It's change I'm looking at. Moment after moment of impermanence. —But I can't call it even that. *It has no unfragmented substance.* When awareness is impeccable, I see in a silent, globed, snowscaped world: rising, sharpness, falling, burning, hearing, tasting, thinking, equanimity. —In this watery seeing I am embalmed in objects. Particles in space dissolving away.

I said to Isaac, "There is light, I am being penetrated by light. This afternoon light was so strong, it sank into my bones. Then my bones dissolved." Isaac nodded. He was looking out the window, away from me. I read:
"Along a shaft of light, dust motes drifted to the left. My head inclined toward them. My lower body expanded. Light sharpened like the point of a knife. It gleamed and broadened. Light turned into breath. Breath cut into my lower back. An icy stream of breath was pulled upward to my shoulders. Beneath my breasts—inside the stem of energy—desire arose. Desire became vibration. The light grew more intense.

"My chest muscles tightened against the intensity of the light.

"Light became a level plane extending outward from my body toward the window. The thin sheet of light interrupted all the sound there was.

"I thought: 'I can't find myself in this.' I watched the arising and passing of the thought. The thought too glinted against my eyes like light.

"When I stood up, my mind was clear."

Isaac said: "What sound? You didn't mention when the sound started. Pay more attention."

I walk back to my room. It is the second time this year I have come to N—— to practice. What good is this teacher?

"In the night there is peril," Isaac said in my dream. "It can't be helped. This is the only reason I am here—to point it out. Now you are closer to it. When you walk away, your head begins to hurt. There's no telling how it will come out. Don't worry. There's nothing you can do. There are signs, but you won't know them. I am here to tell you. Notice the difference between watching and the watcher. The voice that arises in aversion has this function: it arises, as of old, *to protect the self from being dissolved.* As of old. *In fact it is not your voice. Perhaps you think you recognize it. I assure you, you do not."*

"I am walking," I said to Isaac. "Can't you save this for the night?"

Isaac said: "At night I don't concern myself with you."

I continued walking. I thought: "I will do walking meditation in the hall outside my room. I will walk from one end of the hall to another."

When I shifted to my right leg, bliss came—a stream of silver shimmering from a center where I was. My legs began to tremble. I stood still. Bliss subsided. The waves of cool silver fell away. I moved my right leg. Bliss pulsed around me. Each time I took a step, bliss streamed outward. I saw describing would not help me. And describing fell away.

I stood still. My face became bright. Light was burning my face away.

Al said to me: "Only the dead can hear you. Say what you like. I myself make no mention of it to anyone. There are the words you say that can be heard. Isaac listens to these. There are also the words you do not speak. I listen to these. I hold you accountable," Al said. He was standing in a field. Two trees grew out of the center. The field was bordered by white birches. The trees in the center were maple.

I said: "There's a girl who was pointed out to me. I do not think I am qualified to speak for her."

Al said: "If you see the pain is not your *pain, and also not* her *pain, you can speak of it."*

"What else do I need to know?" I asked. "Must I be able to see her face? Must I know about the day she will be married?"

"Don't be ridiculous," Al said. "How on earth could you know these things? You must simply be competent."

I asked, "Can you tell me how?"

"I could," Al said. "In a manner of speaking, I will tell you how to do it."

That evening I walked out to the front of the building. It was early May. A bird's nest had been started on one of the pillars high up. It had just rained. The air was wet. The sun was going down. The evening was cool. I walked farther onto the lawn. Pale yellow tulips called Apricot Beauty were planted in a circle. The tulips were blooming. But it was evening and the blooms were closed. Drops of water lay on the petals made transparent at the tips by the soaking rain. I could see through the edges of the petals. In their invisible centers, the petals were flecked with red. The wet air was still. The fading light made the petals appear more and more fragile and transparent. But along their length I felt them wet and velvety. My hands were cold.

A burst of joy spread through me. How the tulips came to be in the world, or what would become of them, was immaterial. There must be praise for the strange markings. And praise for the unmeaning of the markings. Praise for the translucence. I thought of my own death. I was happy.

The next day I read to Isaac: "A rotating pressure arose in my heart. It moved farther to the left, across my breast as if the flesh were being lifted up and moved. The pressure rose into my throat, to my eyes, upward to my temples, and across my ears, dragged to the left in a circle. Beneath the pressure was moisture. Heat rose into my face. My face began to burn.

"Under the lids of my eyes, deep down, there was sadness. The surface of the sadness was thin, like a pale sheet of ice below which I could see. Under that surface I felt throbbing.

"Along my neck, to the left, energy pulsed from my throat upward.

"There was a connection between the pulsing in my throat, the light, and the sadness underneath the lids. The sadness lay over and darkened the light like a giant cover over a huge bin."

The next morning at 4:30 I ran five miles down the hill to the town, and back. In the dark I could not see the purple azaleas bordering the lawn. I could not see the buds on the two apple trees outside the meditation hall. I could not see the closed tulips ringed in the center of the lawn. I ran in the dark, downhill past the pond on the left. I ran past the

barn with three horses. They had not yet been let out of
their stalls. The ferns on the side of the road were still
close to the earth. The wind was up. I held a scarf against
my mouth. My breath was moist and warm against the
wool.

I read to Isaac:

"There was beating in my throat. There was pulsing in
my cheekbones. The beating rose upward into my temples.
My hands lay against my legs. My legs were *not* my legs."

I looked up from the notebook at Isaac.

"There is only numbness or beating," I said to Isaac.

Isaac's eyes were closed. Then he opened them and
looked at me. I could see his clear brown eyes, incurious,
revealing nothing.

*I do not have a brother, but that night I dreamt my brother had
committed a terrible murder. He had to flee. I accompanied him
in his car. In the middle of the highway stood a man. It was a star-
less night, dark except for the headlights illuminating his shape,
and the broken white line at the center of the road. My brother
struck the man with the car and killed him. A second murder! My
brother took no note. I was the one who noticed. I said nothing. I
sat in the backseat swallowing my terror. When we got to the city
limits, we saw on the left a field dotted with rows of crosses as at
a graveyard. Old Dodges and Plymouths lined the lot in rows. In
my dream we had arrived at a junkyard in dawn light. The sun
was rising over the field of abandoned cars. Next to the junkyard
the highway stretched onward. The pavement was wet. It had just
rained. Oil shone on the surface, pinkish-green with swirls of yellow. We had stopped the car. It was a spring morning, and cold.
I took the wheel now. Near a big city hospital, I was caught. A
policeman stopped the car to question us. My brother's license had
my picture on it. My brother turned me in for the crime. My
brother said: "She did it."*

From the driver's seat, I looked up at the policeman. His eyes were the color of Isaac's eyes. "I'm in the wrong," I said.

The policeman looked bored and said, "Of course you are. But confession doesn't count. Guilt doesn't count."

I read to Isaac: "Light washed through the lids of my eyes. Light spread across my face. The light expanded and contracted in circles. The top of my head grew thin. Light was being poured into it, a wide slow stream of light, expanding as it fell downward. The spot on my head where light funneled down began to throb. There was beating—the pulse of my dying—in my throat, my cheeks, my eyes. Brightness formed in swiftly expanding circles. The edges were rippling and streaming.

"Is this just light from the window coming through my eyelids?" I asked Isaac.

His face was kind and serious. I thought of the word "piteous." I did not know whose eyes they were. The eyes were ancient. His eyes had become what eyes are. He began to speak, then looked sorry. He said, "It's best you go on reading."

I lowered my head and said: "The light is intense. I tighten against it. In the middle of the light there were images of trees—bare trees, but also trees with leaves. The tops of a few trees were stained with lime green; light was shining through the leaves. Isaac, believe me, I only want to see what's there."

"Go on reading," Isaac said.

I read: "Light was coming from the window. My eyes were closed. Light moved across my face, *into* the pores of my face. I noted 'spreading,' 'circling,' 'seeing,' 'waves.' Darkness arose around the light, rimming it. Darkness pierced the center of the light. But also, from within the center of the darkness, a sharper, more acutely focused light radiated so that nothing could be hidden anywhere.

"I moved my attention away from the light, onto 'hearing.' A bird was trilling. I noted 'sound.' The trilling became unintelligible vibration. Vibration shimmered until it too became light. I couldn't find the seam where the vibration from the 'trilling' became 'light.' I couldn't find the 'outside' of the sound *or* of the light. The trilling and the light bled into each other.

"Light poured against my face, onto my neck and shoulders. It fell into my arms. Light seeped into my forearms, then deep into my elbows. Now light broke my arms at the joints. I felt no pain. I shifted my attention again from the light onto the place where my body touched the ground. From that place light expanded outward. I widened the space around the light so that my attention was resting on it from a distance. Attention rested gently on the light.

"When light replaced my face or completely enveloped and obliterated my body, I made my form come back. *I recalled my body*.

"There was beating gently in my chest. There was beating in the palms of the hands, pulsing in my eyelids."

I stopped reading. I asked Isaac: "Am I choosing the objects I see? Or am I passively receiving the objects as they are given to me, without choice?"

Isaac was silent.

"At the end of the sitting," I read, "light covered my face. Light turned in circles and undulated. It moved around the shapes of darkness. I opened my eyes to look at the light coming in the room. Light spilled onto the window sills, but *stopped* at the sills. I closed my eyes. Whenever light grew denser on my face, or when light fell downward into my body, I opened my eyes. Did the light come from outside my body or from inside it? There was no way to know. The light was piteous."

I looked up from my notebook.

"Don't you see I have no reference point?" I asked.

"None whatsoever," Isaac said.

*

"Can I report to you directly?" I asked Al. "After all, isn't it you who really hears me out? Isn't it you to whom I really speak? You for whom I really speak?"

"I'm inaccessible," Al said. "Isaac will hear you out. Isaac is equipped."

"Inaccessible?" I asked. "We're talking—you can't deny that."

Al said, "This arrangement is temporary. You can't speak yourself now. The living never can. I lend you my voice until—"

"Until?"

"Until you have your own."

"Isaac?" I asked.

Al said: "Isaac will always have a voice. He stands between the living and the dead. Isaac is necessary."

"You and I? You will say that we are not necessary."

"That's right," Al said. "Still, I love to watch your hair with sunlight in it. For me, you bring desire. And I—I know you dream of me at night. It is necessity of a kind. I would not like to specify what kind. As I said, it's temporary."

"Isaac?" I asked.

"Isaac doesn't dream," Al said abruptly. "He is beyond it. But for the dead and for the living, dreaming is imperative."

"When will I receive the voice you spoke of?"

"Don't be in a hurry," Al said pensively. "Don't be in a rush. When you have the hang of me, I'll go away."

"You've gone away," I said. "You're dead. You can't go farther."

"I can," Al said.

"And then the voice that's left, the voice that you leave, the voice of the dead—will it be of the dead?"

Al said, "Exactly. That's an open question."

I read to Isaac: "Light came and went across my face. When it began to fall into the breath in those concentric, widening circles, I focused my attention on the breath sensations on my upper lip.

"I'm bored with breath," I said. "I want to speak of pain."
"You *are* speaking of pain," Isaac said.

That afternoon in sitting meditation my attention was
reined in. I observed the breath. Then sound punctured
the breath: operatic, almost continuous, bird sound
from both sides of the room. There was beating in my
chest, head, throat. There was light, taste, smell of the air
coming in the open window, lilac air. I opened my attention. I couldn't note objects fast enough. Sound arose and
stopped. Light sliced through the sensation of beating.
The place of the beating changed. Beating in my wrist,
but not where the pulse is. Beating in my head, drawn upward in a continuous wavering column from the chest.
Everything—beating, light, sound—arose fast and fell
away fast. It fell to the side of consciousness like motes of
dust.

Then thinking arose. I brought attention back to the
breath. Attention was like a rope, a thick, clumsy rope, yet
holding air in. My attention loosened. Mindfulness grew
steady. I turned back to the bird sounds. I heard a wood
thrush calling, or an owl.

I heard hawks screaming high in the air. The sound was
wild, piercing, from another world. I thought: "These
cries will drive me crazy. Listening could make a person
crazy." The sounds fell against each other like thrown
metal rods. All this was new: the tasting, smelling, listening, and the hearing. I felt panic. In the Hall the teacher
struck the great bronze bowl that was our bell. There
were three strokes. Only the last was allowed to prolong
itself, fade, and die. I saw vast spaces. I heard the piercing
cries. I was instructed in meaninglessness by what I heard.
The hawks' call was harsh and random, high up. On some
other plane, *the plane of birds*, maybe something was re-
vealed. But the human world was circumscribed, fenced

by understanding. Attention was a pure register, a white sheet, a long robe.

The voice said: "If you want to speak of pain, you must speak of the body. It's not only sound that troubles you."

I said: "Why do you tell me this? You are neither Al nor Isaac. I can't identify you at all. You have no body."

"Each one has his place," the voice said. "There is the place of the one who is alive (that's you) and of the one who is dead, and of Isaac who stands between. Then there is me. I too have my place."

"Okay," I said. "Then let me tell you this. I am unprotected now. I am unprotected and I am unafraid of dying."

"I doubt that seriously," the voice said.

"I repeat," I said, "I reiterate. I am unprotected by desire, aversion, reason. I'm not saying these aren't present. But these are not protection. And I am unafraid."

"How does it follow?"

"It follows," I said, "as night follows day, etcetera."

"Don't be glib."

I said: "It follows. I have no explanation. I'm trying."

"You're ludicrous," the voice said.

"That too. Abuse me all you want; I'm still trying. I don't know how it follows. I am unprotected and unafraid of dying."

I said to Isaac: "I don't see clearly."

"Read," he said.

I read: "Sadness arose behind my eyes—a piercing archaic, blinding sadness: sorrow. It was not my sorrow. When I stared at it, I grew dizzy. Sorrow deepened. Light spread across my face.

"A tight place arose in my chest. The sensation of gravity pressed against my head, but also against the light outside my eyes and against my arms. An ancient glittering sorrow arose behind my eyes, and behind the lids of my eyes.

"My body was fragile. The whole bone structure was bleached white. My bones were dry and white and clean, as bones in the desert valley are clean, and fragile. Light and breath blew through the bones."

That night I dreamt Al was doing walking meditation in a field of rice. He had his best suit on. It was an expensive brown suit. He said: "The dead have worries. I, for instance. I have my anxieties. I worry most about my body. At the end when I was ill——. Cancer is no joke. Then they cut you open, right through the chest, take out a piece of lung. How do you think that feels? I miss that piece of lung. I don't breathe well. I'm not complaining. I'd like to be dignified, as you think I am. You must know the truth. I dream of my lost lover. He is alive. But how will I be beautiful to him without desire? How have desire without a body? I can tell you, though, how I did it. When I was in my coma, I could hear you. That's no surprise. It is well-known. But if the body can be still like that, still like death, and yet the eardrum functions, there's no knowing. I would weep, but I don't know whether I have eyes."

In the dream, I realized Al was sleepwalking. Al was walking and talking in his sleep. I got up from bed to practice. When I sat down in the meditation posture the skin of my nose was being peeled away. The skin was tingling and burning as it peeled upward.

The next day I said to Isaac: "There is unbearable energy in my calf."

Isaac looked at me. He was deciding whether to comment on the word "unbearable." Isaac was silent. So I said: "Sometimes I think you're not present. Your face looks lifeless. I wouldn't speak to you this way if I had sufficient rest. You don't let me sleep enough. Don't you see that?

——"Okay," I said. "All right. I'll read."

I read: "My calves were being stretched——. The breath was cool, elastic in my calves, falling, stretching downward, being kneaded. I felt 'knotting,' 'pressure,' 'heat' in my ribs when the breath went over them. And soreness arose *between* the ribs.

"Breath came from under the bones I sat on. It was thick in my chest. Breath was floating. The ribs were in the floating, washed by it. Bliss started to come: a silver, green, mercury-like vibration. The soreness faded. Then it changed into a bruise. In the bruised place, between the ribs, bliss spread.

"There was beating in my throat, like a great song."

I said to Isaac, "I am being given trouble in the throat, the calf, the ribs."

"See it neutrally," Isaac said. *"It is just the suffering of the body."*

I read: "My left leg strained to move. I kept still. I noted 'desire.' Desire was in my calf as 'heat,' as an impulse to move. It faded. I noted the same sensation of tingling and burning in the arch of my left foot. This was torment. The inclination to move spread from my calf to the area between the breasts. Desire arose and faded in my chest. I saw it fade. It shifted to the left leg, then to my chest again. There was heat and an explosive pulsing in my chest and leg. In my leg there was a sharp stinging sensation as if I had been bitten."

I turned my eyes to Isaac.

He said: "You are attending closely to the body. Once I decided I would stand still until I learned what produced the intention to move."

Isaac looked beautiful to me. Isaac's body in his long gray pants and beige sweater looked beautiful. "Suffering?" I asked.

"Just so," he said.

I said: "Rapture comes from the body. Rapture, too."

Isaac asked: "Did it not follow?"

"I can tell you this without the notebook," I said. "Desire arose under my eyelids as a gentle rubbing. It arose in the heart area under the beating. It arose in my throat as a stretching of the inside of the throat: as 'pressure,' 'warmth,' 'moisture,' 'pulsing.' Rapture began as 'convulsing,' a sucking in of my belly, as waves of violent sweetness rising in the body and around it, as floating."

Isaac's face looked beautiful to me.

Isaac said: "You'd better read."

I looked down. I found my place and read: "My throat began to pulse. My throat was being sucked back farther into my body. The beating moved to the roof of my mouth. I was choked by a sticky, violent, intense irritation that was sweet and constricting at the same time. On the inward motion there were peaks of undulating warmth. Behind my eyes, behind the moving concentric circles of light, there was sweetness.

"Can't I stop?" I asked Isaac. "Isn't this enough?"

"No," he said. "This is desire. Look at it. Desire is harder to see than suffering."

I felt ill. My pages shamed me. I looked down and read:

"There was beating between my breasts, and a reverberation of beating upward to my collarbone—a low steady hum, close to my body, not touching it. But agitating it. Below the beating, a thin, spikelike pressure was driving down to my belly.

"Light rose upward within my body. The roof of my mouth was dry. I couldn't swallow. A harsher beating arose near the surface of the skin in my left breast below the nipple. The body, inside and outside, was a field caressed.

"Now can I stop?" I asked Isaac.

"What would you prefer to see?" Trese's mother said. She was again in the labor room fussing with the afterbirth. I looked away.

I said: "Not more violence."

"There is violence," Trese's mother said. "Look at me. Look again

at Christa burning on her bed. Of course we needn't look. I used to brush my hair every day. They said I was vain. Say, rather, I was immature. Say I was not maternal: go ahead. I didn't know that beauty doesn't count. You also have a thing or two to learn on that score. I could brush and brush my reddish hair, so beautiful with sunlight in it. I swung it to and fro and brushed."

I laid down on Trese's mother's gurney. Night falls. She lies dead by my side, still in her white hospital gown, still messy from the birth. She says: "Someone should comfort you, but I can't do it."

"Yesterday," I told Isaac, "I saw the inside of my throat. I felt the pain from which no body is ever free. *I felt it as the beating.* Now it is in my heart, and my jaw is being pushed toward my throat and locked in place by two throbbing points of pain that reach from the center of both cheeks to my neck. My jaw is wedged open. Also, there is a band of steel wires around my neck.

"Screws tightened the wires around my neck between four points, two under my ears and two in my upper back. Between my head and back, the neck bulged at the points where the screws tightened."

Isaac said: "I think you're minding the pain less."

I said: "Because I see the pain in more detail. *I see it now precisely.*"

*

That night, late, I went into the Meditation Hall. I was restless. My knees hurt. My back was stiff. I had knelt in the meditation posture for nine hours since 4:30 that morning. I went to the back of the room and sat in an empty chair. The lights were off in the room, except for a light far away on the Buddha. Blankets lay on the long rows of meditation cushions stretching away in front of me: folded blankets, blankets heaped beside cushions, blankets formed into walled circles. All day blankets had been wrapped around legs, around waists, around torsos. All day blankets held bodies. Now the blankets were cast aside and the bodies were gone.

I held my blanket around my shoulders. The vast room was cold. I was awake and restless. Far away outside I heard crickets. May was early for crickets. I closed my eyes. The room was still. Suddenly I had a sense of not knowing where I was.

I opened my eyes. I said out loud: "I don't know where I am." The room was vacant, dark, haunted, ancient. Until now the room had concealed its vital life. This was a room I hadn't seen before. I couldn't make sense of it. I looked coldly in front of me. I looked judiciously, as if someone were watching me deliberate. My mind was dark. "I don't know where I am." In a corner far away at the bottom of awareness, a crack of fear appeared and widened. But I was also curious. Instantly I remembered everything. It was a room that I knew well.

I thought, "I must be tired. I must be stupid with concentration to be confused like this." I was alert. I walked slowly back toward my room, carrying my body as if it were an injured stranger. I guided myself with my hand along the wall. The texture of the wall was grainy, cool. As I walked, I had the sense that my body was held upright by a force that wasn't my own. The blue blanket, three books by the bed, one glass for water, the shoes, a pen and the notebook I write in. "To recognize," I wrote. "I *recognize*." The word has three syllables. I lay down, turned off the light, and fell asleep in my clothes.

The next day I told Isaac: "I didn't know where I was."

Isaac looked interested. He said: "Tell me about the mind-moment directly before the not-knowing occurred."

I couldn't find a memory for the moment he asked about. I had been sitting in my chair. I'd heard the crickets. Then there was a space, a gap. Nothing was *in* the gap. If there was something there, I couldn't see it. I tried again to think: the chair, the crickets, the blankets, the intention to sit. I was afraid. I said: "I can't tell you that."

Isaac looked triumphant.

Al said: "I had to lie in the box a long time before the flesh rotted. Some say it's not so long. I disagree. The Jews have a prohibition against cremation. Say, at least, they're squeamish. They want the body buried, preferably. To what end?—I lay there and lay there, uncomfortable. I had a twin who died when I was seven. You recall the photo of us in the sailor suits? I lay in the box and thought of him. The body is no good—you'll get no argument from me. But what else is there? I didn't suffer. I just thought of my twin. I never spoke of him, why should I now? I was so nervous when I was alive. All my life I couldn't drive. I thought I'd killed him that way. When my mother put me to bed, I knew she missed him. She would kiss my forehead, thinking of him. I like to think of him dry-eyed, a little boy who died in his sleep. There is no grief here, so there can be none for him. Still, I've never seen him. No memory and no grief, no being at all. I keep some of my habits, though," Al said. "I still read with my glasses. I still sleep restlessly. And I like to make a scene. *The body can be cremated or buried. I myself favor fire. I'll tell you what is most important. Not to second-guess things. For instance, I say 'when my lover comes. . . .' The truth is, I don't know. They speak of the resurrection of the body. Frankly, I haven't seen it. For worms, perhaps. But not for us. I would have preferred cremation. Then the living would have seen what the body is worth. Be certain: I can't find my twin here."*

That evening I thought about the death of the flowers. When I began this period of practice three weeks ago there were tulips and daffodils. Leaves came to the apple boughs. Then blossoms came to the apple trees, pale. Nothing could last looking like that. The blossoms fell off. Then came tiny blossoms that widened into conelike structures, lacy and dappled with red. And bluet, inch-tall white upright star-shaped flowers, blooming in the grass. Lilacs came that are now dying. Iris bloomed a few days ago. They did not last more than a day inside. On their first day fully open, they looked alive as animals are alive. The peonies in the garden were sticky with sap, about to bloom. Along the road the low ferns were lush and huge.

I said to Isaac: "The vise, in which my attention has been holding, clutching, and making objects captive, is beginning to loosen."

Isaac was sleeping. He was dreaming of fields of blue poppies. He lay on the sand by the ocean. He lay on his side. His arm was stretched over his head. His body in black trunks was cool and white. The sun had gone in. Goose bumps were on his flesh. I put my hand on his chest to warm him.

Isaac said in his sleep: "I am having a bad dream. The poppies take my oxygen. They are very beautiful. Do you see them blowing in the breeze? Look at the petals. See the texture? You can't look through it. Of course, light filters through. That's what encourages you to think it's possible to see to the other side. But if you get very close, you'll note that you can't do it. Then, of course, there is the yellow center of the poppy. I have stared at that a long time. I fear the stamen."

"Well, then, look away," I said to Isaac. "There are other things to see. For instance, there is the water. Surely you hear how the waves explode on the beach. Now they are very loud. Don't you hear that? Can't you look at that? Look at your own white body. —You could look at me. I am leaning over you, curious."

Isaac said: "Don't distract me."

I said: "What if I looked at the yellow center of the poppy, too."

"To me that is a matter of complete indifference," Isaac said.

"Anyway, you would not see the same yellow center that I see. Then, too, your eyes would be dazzled by the intense, grainy yellow. I don't think you could look very long. But my attention is unwavering."

"What do you see?" I asked Isaac.

"I see the center of the poppy," Isaac said. "I see the whole life of the center of the poppy at one glance. Although the poppy is in its first bloom, I see the center of the poppy decay. As I look, the little filaments are curling and drying out. Death is different for each creature that dies, and that difference is important. One might, without practice, be inconsolable."

"And persons? What happens when you look at them. Did you never look?"

"If I look at you, it is no help. You will be old soon. You are old now," Isaac said. "If I look through you, I see the others."

"What others?" I had put my head on his shoulder.

"The countless ones. The grandmother. Your lovers. The ones that are in your eyes. Now I will tell you something in translation," Isaac said. "The more you look at the center (the intense yellow), the more pain you feel in your eyes. Tears are shallow and dry up. Everyone knows that."

I began to kiss him. "Is this useless?"

"Not at all," he said. "Still, there is the center of the poppy. If you looked at it (at another particular one) with the same burning—looked at everything about it in the finest moment of its dying—with love, I would let you go home. But there are things you must be able to tolerate."

"Pain?" I asked.

He didn't answer. He rather said: "It is possible to think this: without a reference point there is meaninglessness. But I wish you'd understand that without a reference point you're in the real."

I pushed Isaac down in the sand. His body fell easily. I began to pour sand into his eyes, and into his mouth which was still talking. I poured sand into the hollows of his neck. When his whole face was covered, I lay on top of him and slept.

*

In the afternoon I went for a walk. It had just rained and the air was heavy with moisture. The sky had brightened. I was discontent. I was walking downhill. On the road about six feet ahead I saw an animal. It looked freshly dead. Long and vital, but unmoving. I couldn't see the wound that killed it. Its fur was beautiful, sleek and full. I saw its fur glisten, ruffled as if by wind. The air was still. The animal was stretched out, its head pointing in one direction, feet in another. It must have been killed running. The tail with its tufts of grays and browns curled slightly upward and was textured like a rich wool. I was fascinated by the intactness of the body. I said to myself: "I won't look at it now. On the way *back* from my walk, on the way *uphill*, I will look at it."

Returning up the hill, my thoughts were of the dead animal. When I had seen it for the first time it looked perfect, whole. I don't know what killed it. I said to myself: "Did I see it dead or did I see it in the most vital moment of its life? Am *I* dead? Am I in the most vital moment of my life? Dharma has killed the animal. Dharma will kill me."

I had not reached the top of the hill. Walking up the hill was more difficult than walking down it. I tried to keep my attention in the present, but my thoughts returned to the animal, languorous, dead, but vital, stretched out on the road, eyes looking upward. I arrived again at the place where I had seen it. The road was bare. I walked back and forth looking for the body, the carcass, the thick-furred, sensuous animal. I was certain it *had* been here. But it was nowhere I looked.

Perhaps it had been run over again. Perhaps the animal that lay vibrantly dead across the pavement when I walked downhill had been crushed and erased. Perhaps it had been taken up by a hawk. I walked back and forth where it had appeared to me. I saw nothing.

Can attention grow so refined that it could hold an object out of time in vision—freeze it—even while it was moving? Maybe at the moment I had seen it dead, the animal was running.

The body was no impediment. I was open without boundary to the rest of the world. A thought arose like a spark from a match. It flickered and disappeared: Where thought was, here the world is now.

That night I dressed in the dark. I kept my eyes open. I looked forward to my interview with Isaac. I would ask him matter-of-factly about my day. Tonight there would be comfort in reading him entries from my notebook. I considered which entries I would read him, if we were pressed for time.

Later that night I knocked on Isaac's door for my interview. He looked at me reflectively. I sat down on my chair across from him and opened my notebook. Before I could start reading Isaac began to speak. He said: "I think, after all, we will *not* meet tonight."

The next morning when I sat for the first meditation period, I felt as if I were being held upright. I had no difficulty keeping my back straight. It was being held *for* me. My body sat in its space as if it barely displaced air, as if it were suspended. I could feel a slight swaying at the shoulders where the displacement of the air occurred.

That afternoon I again took a walk. A cry came out of my body as if I had never seen that animal's corpse before. One of the paws was bent forward at the first joint. There was a drop of blood in the place of the upturned eye. There was blood at the mouth. I stood over the animal for a few minutes looking at it. The eyehole cupped the blood

which had congealed in that spot. I thought about touching it, but I was afraid. This time it was not beautiful.

On the way back up the hill again I saw a *living* animal,
as alive as I am, in a stone wall to my right. It looked directly at me. It went in and out of the crevices of the wall,
stopping to peer at me. Often its body was hidden, but I
could see its bright eye. This one was alive and real. This
one I now looked at was hyperalive as the one the day before had been hyperdead. I was being shown something.
The animal's bright eye reappeared at the crevice of the
stone wall. Then the whole body of the animal appeared
and stood for a moment looking at me.

Coiled up right here in the live one was the dead one.

In meditation the next hour after my walk, the bee sound
began, as if it were the sound of awareness. After a while
the sound stopped. The room was still. My attention was
directed to a spot below my shoulder blades. There was
pressure and burning in that spot. The words "Something
isn't right" formed in my mind. Beating, the storyless pain
from which no body is ever free, arose in my heart. Again
the words formed: "This isn't right." I heard a metallic
noise, as if something had fallen directly in front of me. At
the other end of the room a door closed. Space was collapsed between the door and my body. The sound was at
hand. Things far away were not far away. Places that are vacant and places that are filled are the same.

Then dharma struck my body and pushed it down. I had
the sensation of density without form. Dharma pushed me
down. I was rotated from the left to the right. My neck
was uprooted. It was carefully pulled out of the shoulder
blades as if it were a stem. Where there is no agent there
is perfect care. In dharma is utmost violence and utmost
care.

*

After tea when I sat in meditation, the beating was fast in the area of my heart. Not the image but rather the sense of my body as a skeleton came and hovered around me. The sense settled in. In my back only the shell of my body remained. Some bones were left in place, some misplaced: the clavicle, the pelvis, a segment of spine. My body had grown utterly strange. The front was carved out, and space flowed freely through the rib cage, flowed beautifully between the places where bones still held up and where others had collapsed. The bones lay disarranged but peaceful like a shipwreck that has been under water for many years and the currents have scattered the timbers of the wreck for miles across the ocean floor.

When I woke very early the next morning the room looked strange. The dark was fading. It was a June morning, early. Shapes looked flat, one-dimensional. I stood up and began dressing for my morning run. My legs felt uncoordinated as I dressed. I put on my watch and checked the dial, but I could not read it. I saw a round circle with radiating spokes. I looked again, and then again until I saw the spokes were really intelligible positions of the hands of the watch. "Time" returned.

Sunrise. The night dews were still on the grasses, on the stones of the fences, on the paving of the road. I had been running for a while when I grew confused about whether I had passed the road on which I turn left or whether I was yet to pass it. I ran on not knowing, and not recognizing where I was. I came to the turn. I did remember it, and went left at the field of corn. Again, after a while I couldn't recall having seen these fields before with hay rolled into bales at the center of them. In a bit I passed the flattened body of the animal I had seen yesterday. The eye-hole was berrylike, again full of fresh blood. How could that be? I stopped to look at it. I must have been mistaken about the place where it was killed. I thought it had been run over before the brown house on the left, but the animal in fact lay far down the road. I had the sense that nothing could harm me now. Death is not harm. I felt fearless, and clear.

The sun was getting higher.

I ran uphill now. I was breathing hard. I ran past the barn on my right looking for a certain barking dog. But after a moment of confusion, I saw I had already *passed* the farm where the dog lived. I ran faster and tried to think. "Before" and "after" are imaginary designations, ways I have of separating parts of experience from other parts. In fact there *are* no parts. The parts really happen simultaneously. That was one possibility. The other was that I thought something *had* come when it hadn't *yet* come, or that it was *going* to come when it *had come* because there are gaps in consciousness, moments in which there is *no being at all*.

Isaac asked about the mind-moment directly preceding the one in which I didn't know where I was. I couldn't tell him. If there were gaps in consciousness, where was I *during* them? The night before when I had taken my clothes off to shower I had looked in the mirror, and through my chest I saw ribs. I saw the body of my death.

Now the sun was higher. I could see it on my right glinting off the lake. The dew on the grasses along the road was gray and silver, beaded as it lay on the sloped fields to the left. The air was dry. I ran faster. A voice (my own voice) said: "This is beautiful work."

After the first meditation period of the morning, when the sun was almost overhead, I went outside to the road where there is an oak tree and a maple tree. The road from one tree to the other is flat. In the direction of the town I can see where the hill slopes downward. On the other side of the road is a row of chestnut trees. Wind is blowing chestnut blossoms onto the street. Beneath a chestnut tree, pale yellow butterflies fly in and out of lilac bushes. Blossoms still hang on some of the branches.

My course was thirty paces long. As I walk, the road begins to rise up and crumble under my feet. The pavement is cracking and buckling. Destruction rises from within it and breaks the pavement into dangerous pieces, into volcanic rocks, tossed on top of each other in a ruin. Now the sun is directly overhead. I recognize, at a distance, Louis, my grandfather, coming toward me. He can walk on the heaving pavement easily, even though it collapses under his feet. Louis says as he approaches: "Time *does* this to a road, Annie."

In the middle of my path I stood still. I looked up at the trees. The wind was blowing. The wind was green and blowing. Suddenly I saw into the leaves. They were far above me, but close up. They were magnified, huge, changing color with great speed while I looked. I was looking at leaves rushing toward their own extinction. I saw, through the blowing, the turning of the lush green leaves to red ones. The green ones *contained* the red ones and already *were* them. The leaves were turning and blowing while I looked. Wind was roaring in the trees at a distance. The wind widened as it approached. I stared into the trees above me. I could barely see. The colors of the world bled into each other. Greens paled into grays and whites. The backs, the underside of the leaves, tossed and blew. Silver glittered coldly in the light. Then the wind quieted. Louis said: "This is death. It will frighten you less and less."

*

That afternoon I walked to the Meditation Hall past the apple tree and the peonies. A sweet bush, honeysuckle, throws its perfume into one of the back windows of the Hall. By the stone wall at the bottom of the driveway iris blooms. I can see the dark purples on the inside of the flower. Lavender petals curl upward. The silky peonies are cream-colored, with ragged edges where the seams have split, magenta, like blood stains on white fabric. Grass recently cut. The air is dry and light. My body is transparent. Light from the midday sky glints through it at an angle. Joy arises. The joy is outside in the air like the iris's cool lavender rising around the midnight-blues. The edges of the joy are crisp. This was a different sweetness than the grass or honeysuckle. This had evolved from the milky insides of the pain-seed's fruit.

I feel sad. I noted it behind the lids of my eyes. It fell away. Sadness arose in my chest. It fell away. Nothing was left.

I walked to my meditation cushion and sat. What I called "sadness" was a sequence of sensations in the lids of my eyes, in the area of my heart, in this sharpness or that burning, separate, discontinuous sensations that the word "sadness" obscures. Each time the emotion I called "sadness" arose, I lifted it up in my hand and looked at it, turning it this way and that. I am at work on "sadness." The sensations were discontinuous. This was also true for "impatience," and "tiredness." It was true for "thought." Thought tried to make sadness solid. Thought itself was an arrow in the mind. My body was taken up by a benevolent force. But there was no reason for fear.

Al was lying in a field of corn. He was sleeping. I parted the corn stalks and kneeled beside him. The soil on my knees was damp.

"I am seeing the ending of things," I said.

Al continued sleeping.

"I am speaking to you," I said. But the tassels of the corn blew over his eyes and the long green leaves covered his face. I could tell by looking at it that the corn was almost ripe.

"I have something to tell you," I said. "It can't wait."

Al slept on.

"All right," I said. "Two can play that game." I lay down beside him, and folded my arms against my chest, as if I were dead. Next to me, I could feel Al breathing.

"I have a thing or two to ask you. Are you of the opinion that I can learn to do this by myself? I honestly don't see how," I said.

Across the field I could see through the stalks of corn. The green and straw-colored tassels glittered. Above, the sky had bright stars in it, although it was still day. I looked at the stars. I grew afraid.

"If you won't talk to me, I'll talk to myself," I said. I was silent.

Then I heard a plow at the edge of the field of corn. The plow began to excavate the ground, even though corn was already standing in long gleaming rows, even though stars shone on the corn.

"Stop," I screamed. "Don't you see two people are sleeping here? Or that a crop is fruiting? Any fool could see this is hallowed ground." The plow did not stop. I heard it at the very edge of the field, turning up deep furrows of earth, exposing the roots of the corn.

"We'll be destroyed," I said to Al. I got up on my elbow and looked down on him, but his sleep was deep and dreamless. I could see nothing.

I stood up and took his two feet in my hands and tried to drag the body to the side, away from where I could see the plow would eventually drive its blade through earth, but I could not move him.

"Give me directions," I said, "or tell me how to wake you."

The plow was getting closer. In the sky the stars flashed. Then they burned, cooled to a cloud of ice, broke into pieces, and began to fall.

That night when I tried to sleep, the loud bee-sound arose. It was buzzing and teeming close to my ear. My head turned into space. The bee-sound strengthened. My head disappeared into the space around it. *There was no sin-*

gle consciousness to unify what happened. There was hearing-consciousness, seeing-consciousness, feeling-consciousness, thinking-consciousness. These states of consciousness were distinct from each other like shiny beads on a string, polished beads set so close to each other I could barely see the beads were separate pieces. But not like that at all. Nothing, no filament, held the beads together. This is why Isaac closed his eyes when I spoke. Isaac knew this.

"If you had the sense you were born with," my grandmother said, "I'm telling you. . . ." She was gardening, forty years ago. A scarf was tied over her head. She wore a gingham sundress. She had beautiful legs. She was comfortable in her body. She knew she looked good. Even bent over the dirt, she looked elegant. Her back and arms were tan. When she wiped her arm across her brow, I saw the arc her body made: lean and tight and hard. When she leaned over farther, light caught the hem of her dress. Now I could see that under the gingham the backs of her legs were brown and smooth. It was summer. She was pulling at the beets. But the beets weren't coming. The greens were breaking off in her hand. When her earrings caught the light, they glittered.

"Telling me what?" I asked. I sat to the side of the garden. She had her back to me, bending over the beet greens. She was impatient, trying to get the plants to come up whole. I loved my grandmother's summer body.

"My Sol died in the war," she said. "He was shot down over Germany the day Germany surrendered. I am making borscht. Even if I can't get the beets out of the ground, I'll make it. They never found his body."

"My mother told me."

My grandmother turned from her digging to look at me. "What does she know?"

"See the dirt under my nails?" she said. "I couldn't bury him. I love you best, after Sol. Pick the dirt off the beets. Can you do this for me?"

"The beets are underground," I said.

"Never mind. I've been digging and digging for years. I want to come to the place where the body is. It must be somewhere. Listen, if I knew I had to die, I'd do it differently." She laid a beet leaf next to me. "I wouldn't have spent twenty years grieving for Sol. I wouldn't have chased your grandfather out of my room, or put rags between my legs so he couldn't enter me. This is what I would have done," she pulled the scarf off her head, and shook her long brown hair out. My grandmother was beautiful.

She sat down on the grass and brushed the dirt off her hands. "I think," she said, "I would have taken a lover." She put her hands along the sides of her bodice and smoothed them downward. I could see the outline of her nipples. She said: "I know I would."

"And when you die, what shall I do?" I asked my grandmother.

"Can you dance?" she asked.

I shook my head, "No."

"Then make me a few words. Tell about the night your grandfather came to me in Russia. We were sixteen. We had our pictures taken under the maple tree. In the early evening we went into the woods and lay in the autumn leaves. We took off all our clothes and he caressed me."

The next morning when I woke, a sharp, burning sensation drove into the arch of my foot. "All right," I said. I stood up.

When I sat in meditation there was "beating" and "humming." "Heat" arose out of the "humming." It moved downward into my feet. I put my right hand to my right foot. I jerked my hand away. My foot was burning. Vertigo. Words arose: "the vertigo is from the extreme disconnection of the sensations." Words fell away. "Is from," "Is from," I repeated. Nothing is holding this together.

The beating quickened. It was wearing a path outward from my throat, through the flesh, to my neck. The disconnectedness—of the beating, the pulse, the pressure, the ripples, the hardness—made this unendurable. My body and this energy imploding had nothing to do with each other. It will go on like that: this pulsing strung through my sentient body.

I was on the verge of seeing. I couldn't see.

In the next meditation period I heard the humming, the sound of life. "What is that? What is that?"

During the "humming" I saw the vast body system. Without my willing anything, cogs of various diameters turned in spite of me. I could hear the metal wheels going around and around at many different velocities. The sound of the whirring wheels became cacophonic. You could see how the whole thing worked, *if* you could *see* the whole thing. I couldn't. In successive moments there was a spasm, a thought, a tightening, an in-breath, aversion, turning. The turning was like a buzzing and humming inside a fermenting vat.

*

The meditation instructions that I follow are the same as they have always been: "Watch the arising and passing away of things. When your attention is not clear, use a mental note to sharpen the mind." The same instructions. But today I *see* differently.

I see the breast bone is broken. The rib cage is turned outward to the world.

I see the entity that is "myself" break up and crumble. Then I see the piece of myself I call "thinking." "Thinking" is independent of any consciousness, which is individual and intentional. "Thinking," "touching," "swallowing," "tasting," "seeing," "hearing" are separate as drops of rain are separate. As geese flying are separate. As leaves from trees of different species lie along the ground and are separate. As the dead are separate from one another and from the living.

In my body, form is broken up by the chaotic dispersal of the buzzing, rippling energy.

The bee-sound of the streaming energy moves from left to right. *I am not solid*.

In the last sitting of the day I heard a *narrow* hum: a different energy, more tunnel-like than the round, expansive buzzing. Eventually another hum from my left ear came to consciousness. It was lower still and concentrated like the sound of a swarm of bees in a lilac bush.

I am telling you the whole thing, as I can see it. There were these three streams of energy: the narrow hum of the universe, the note this body made, and a third mysterious hum. There were no feelings. There was equanimity, and happiness. It was a relief to see nothing but this mechanical process, these sounds at three frequencies.

The beating had thinned out. The energy unknotted and spilled throughout my body.

The bee-sound drenched my head with streaming. It surged under the sitting bones and widened in my groin. It pulsed along my shoulders and down my arms. It was sweet and powerful, not ominous. It was not menacing, only strong. My body burned.

I said to Isaac: "During meditation, impressions register, but not deeply. In meditation, my body is a surface. It has no depth."

Isaac yawned.

"I say they don't register," I continued. "There is nothing for them to register *on* except awareness."

"Why don't you read," Isaac said.

"In a minute. It's disconcerting to see my body permeated by energies, inside and outside of it, more disconcerting than to see space *replace* the body. The body is conserved, but it's disarticulated as material substance, and then made up again of immaterial energies. When space *consumes* my body and there is no more body, I think it is uncanny. But when my body is unmistakably there, I know this is how it ordinarily is, even though it is no longer composed as body, but permeated with light.

"So—I'm telling you—the body is composed of energies, and feelings of different pressures. I had a thought about this, but it vanished."

I looked at Isaac. His eyes were closed. I said: "Won't you tell me anything I want to know?"

"Not a thing," he said.

"And when I go home?"

"Oh, you'll come back," he said. "You'll keep coming back."

I looked at Isaac. His face looked like snow.

I sat in a field of snow. Snow numbed my bare legs, which were stretched in front of me. I had only shorts on and a summer top. Ahead a wild rose bush grew next to a pointed rock. The rock was ochre and blue. The rock and the wild rose bush were far away. Herons flew against the horizon, and the sky—shading to violet and gray in the distance—brightened against the earth rim like a sky that's clearing after a long rain. I thought there might be a rainbow. There was no rainbow.

"We were all expecting it," the voice said. "Don't you think it's balmy?"

"I don't think anything," I said.

"It's time that you begin," the voice said. "Thinking never hurt."

"I can't see," I said. "My legs are frozen. The glare off the snow is terrific. If I close my lids, I feel them against my eyes. They hurt. Open or closed it's the same."

"Make a story of it," the voice said. "Embellish. It helps a little. I'm not saying it helps much. But if for instance there are characters, there must be a plot. So much can happen if you're lost in that."

"You're not an authority," I said. "I have my own views."

"But you can't state them," the voice said. "Of this I have no doubt."

I looked at the snow. It was banked to my left and glittered. Against it there was a glacier and, around it, a cold glacial stream. There was the rock, too, next to which the wild rose bush grew. The edges of the roses fluttered. So there was also wind. "I can't state them," I agreed.

"And so," the voice said, "I make my point. In those conditions, people have been known to freeze. No telling, too, what happens to the mind."

"If I look at the sky," I said, "I will be certain. Either there'll be the light that burns away at my eyes, or there will be the weight of my lids."

"I'm telling you, it's pointless," the voice said.

"Completely pointless," I said.

When I sat that afternoon thinking *arose*. Thinking blotted out awareness. Thinking was the release of certain electrical impulses, like a spasm or a twitch that resulted accidentally in a thought. Thinking came from the firing of neurons. When awareness didn't rise up to meet the thought, the thought was bent by its nature to substitute a false world for a true one.

I saw the mechanical nature of these sensations: sounds, noises, thoughts, waves rising in my chest, moisture and tightness when swallowing. A spasm of energy pulsed through my left foot, cramping the toes. The energy kneaded my foot with its own design and purposes.

I felt affectless. There was no place for affect to be located. In the place where a self *was,* I saw the contraption of the apperceptive mechanism shaking itself to pieces. "Disappointment" when I looked at it with this kind of sight was only this pressure or that burning.

I heard the hum and the bee-sound constantly. And for a few mind-moments, I felt liberated. *Hearing this changed everything.*

Something, right now, prevented me from dying. I was a clear bottomless glass through which there was continual pouring. I felt it was the pouring that preserved my life.

Now thinking arose again like a glinting blade. Awareness was gone. The serrated blade ripped away at nothing. I can't tell you how long the sawing lasted. After the sawing finished, a film spread over my mind and clouded it up. Awareness arose again. The film lifted. *Thinking and awareness do not exist simultaneously.* And when they do—it seems they sometimes do—awareness is a light that *shines* on thinking, illuminating *what thinking is.*

It was absurd to say "I am" ("I am thinking," "I am happy") about any part of this mechanical process. The thought "This is degrading" rose into my mind. The thought splintered.

Awareness alone is not mechanical. I cannot say what awareness is. Awareness is nothing. *Is no thing.*

"The voice asked:"What would you *do with a voice, if you had it?"*

I was lying under a pile of rubble. There was dust in my eyes. Needless to say I couldn't speak. My throat was almost closed. When I breathed, dust motes hit the back of my throat. The taste was chalky in my mouth. It may be the dead lay around me. For sure they did. My teeth were covered with plaster. Plaster lay over my head where the sky should have been.

"If you had a voice to speak of pain, and it were just *a voice, you couldn't trust it. Not to mention: who would listen? If it were more than a voice, if it were pain* and *a voice, then perhaps. But*

*if you saw it was not your pain and not your voice, there might
be a chance."*

*I turned under the rubble. I was on my belly. My face lay against
the plaster. Somewhere there would be nails, but I couldn't feel
them. The plaster dust was light. I moved my arms and legs against
the plaster dust as if it were snow.*

*"Not only that," the voice continued, "you'd find conditions in-
tolerable. You'd want to be unconscious. If you could speak (and
I'm not saying you can), there'd be pain in any case. There'd be the
light in the eyes or the lids against them, or something else. And
no choosing which. Let's not waste words or be equivocal."*

*From above me, I thought I heard sounds, but I couldn't tell. My
throat was almost closed. If I couldn't swallow soon, I would choke.*

*"And then you'd have nothing to say. Let's face it. The best know
that, and you're hardly the best. At best, at best. . . ." The voice
broke off.*

*I began to swallow the plaster dust. If I took a small enough
mouthful, I could manage. If I chewed it, I would be sure to spit
out the nails, if there were nails. My eyes were closed and my face
was turned to one side. The wind will come and blow the dust
away.*

*"It won't do that," the voice said calmly. "You won't be in the
clear. If you're going to speak, it will have to be from there. I can't
tell how you'll breathe. That's not my business."*

*Or the rain will come and wash away the plaster dust. Or
mouthful after mouthful I will swallow it.*

*"Not that either," the voice said brightly. "And so there's
nothing——"*

Isaac was noncommittal. His feet were pushed out in front
of him. "Why would you want to speak?"

"Speaking helps me see pain isn't owned."

He considered. "Start with a joke. Why not?"

"I don't *know* any jokes.——I don't think you know any
either."

"Start with the sweetness."

"Where shall I put it?"

"You must put it where it *is*. Definitely," Isaac said firmly.

"How shall I end?"

"End with a joke. *And put me in it!* Or with the bee-sound."

Isaac stood up and stretched. I could see past him out the window to the lawn. It was two o'clock in the afternoon.

Al said: "Why did you choose me to see you through? There are other dead."

I said: "Ten days before you died, I sat with you. You slept off and on. Your mouth was filled with sores. I gave you apple sauce. We sat across from each other at the kitchen table."

"That's why?" Al said.

"We barely talked."

"Why?" Al said.

"You saw your dying clearly. *You looked at it continuously. You saw* it *alone was real. Your face was beautiful. It was flushed a little. The lines were smoothed away. Your cheek was warm.*

"Five days later I sat in your hospital room. You hadn't moved since they brought you in. You were in your coma. The nurse came to turn you. I asked: 'Can he hear us?'

"She said: 'Sure, he can. He's just sleeping. How do you feel, Al?'

"You didn't move. Then you said from the bottom of your coma, 'Just wonderful.'"

*

Al was standing with the light in back of him. He had his jacket off. He had his glasses on. But he wasn't reading. There was nothing behind him except light. His hair (blond) was combed back from his forehead. The lines on his face were smoothed out. His tan shirt was open at the neck. He held a bookmark in his hand.

Al said: "It's come to this. We can't do better. And I could say a thing or two to make that clear. I have been walking and walking, thinking it through. My legs trouble me at night. The nights are long, let me tell you. Alone as I am—for be assured I am alone —I think of my lover. There is his death to worry about. Not to mention yours. I mean to see this through. Of course, it does no good to worry. Worry is ill-founded. Then again, I think: if the nights are too long (for him I mean), how will he manage? The least thing makes him irritable. And if he doesn't have the necessary patience, well—"Al's voice broke off. "You too," Al said. "That goes for you. You at least can hear me."

"He can't?" I asked.

"No," Al said. "These are the conditions. I take them as they're given. You must do that too."

"I don't know what they are," I said.

Al said: "I think you do."

Al began to walk in the open space. The light around his body was beautiful. It was five o'clock in the afternoon. The air was growing chilly. Al walked several paces, turned around and walked back. He had gym shoes on. His hands were clasped behind his back. I saw that he was thinking. His blue eyes looked intensely at the light. Sun shone on his mustache, paling it. Al, walking, sure looked distinguished!

"If the sun goes down," Al said, "as of course it will, you should turn your eyes to the sky. The birds will be flying across it. Cranes. There is that to see. It's not negligible. Then there is the light. If you look off to the blue, you will see the light grow watery. Keep looking as the color fades. Do that. When even the yellow washes out to white, keep looking. I can't say if there will be stars. But if the sky is clear, there will be stars."

"Are you giving me instructions, Al?" I asked.

"I am," he said.

"Then let me say flat out: Pain deepens."

"Think of the dead. Think how pain is for us, for me, I mean, for I'm the only one I speak for."

"I think you speak for others."

"*Think what you like,*" Al said: "*It deepens.*"

"*What should I do?*"

"You must look. *You might think you see a cause for pain. As, for example, the girl in the locked room did. But even she discerns little difference between one side and the other of the locked door, though, for the sake of argument, we'll say it would be better if the door were open.*

"*Look at the cause,*" he continued, "*as if it were a crane flying across the evening sky.*

"*Look when the night comes and it grows cold. You won't be adequately clothed. I'm sorry. If you start to weep, see that they are glass tears, beautiful but made of crystal. Sing yourself a song. I could do it for you if I were there, but I won't be there.*

"*If there are snows (for one can never tell), you'll want to lie down and put your arm across your face. If the snow should fall against your eyelashes and into the corners of your eyes, don't, by any means, be alarmed. The night, I fear, is long.*"

"*I can't do this,*" I said. "*I can't.*"

"*No.*" Al said, "*Why not?*"

"*Why should I?*"

"To see pain clearly. *As you look, you'll grow* gifted. *You'll come to have capacity.*"

"*And the others? Where will the others be?*"

"*I can't take care of everything. I have my own death to manage.*" He paused, and then continued. "*There will be others. You don't think it's only* your *pain you see? When your eyes begin to burn, use your ears. Hear all the dumb voices buried in the night. If you are very still you will hear* this *cry and that murmuring. You may hear the silent ones best. If the wind comes up, as it might, the leaves will stir. That is the sweetest music! We don't* have *trees* here." *Al put his jacket on.*

The winds came up, and a crow began to make its noises. The night had fallen. I put candles all around. Then the voice said: "What are you *doing here?"*

"I am trying to get into the space where Al is, and where Trese's mother is."

The voice said, "That's impossible. Do you hear the animal crying in the wall? That's the closest you can get. It has been dying a long time. It's hysterical and calm, by turns. Do you hear it?"

"I don't hear anything. I want to be where Trese's mother is, and Al. And Christa."

"You can't do that," the voice said. "First there is the problem of the body. Then——I'll be candid——you don't know enough. Third, you're not allowed. Fourth, you are in the same space. Can you realize, realize?" the voice said. "I'll bet you can't. For instance, look how you squander speech. Then, too, all the time you spend imagining. To be in the same space——Why? What would you do?"

I said: "I would break through the wall and find the dying animal. I would make sure the candles didn't flicker. I would study my hand. I would see what it could do and what it could not do. I would be capable. I would listen to what the dead say. If certain changes were necessary——"

"Yes?" the voice said.

I was silent.

The voice said: "You must place your ear to the floor and listen."

Then I was in the vestibule. It was only moments before Al's death, and before my grandmother's death, and before Trese's mother's death. Al was in his coma. My grandmother was forming words, but the stroke had taken away her speech. Trese's mother was in the labor room. All of them were tired. I put my hand to the glass wall at the end of the vestibule and found the place where the glass melted into air. Then I climbed over the glass wall and stood directly in front of them.

Trese's mother is the most mysterious, and she knows it. Someone has combed out her long red hair for her. She wants to know if the baby looks like her. Then she remembers the baby isn't born *yet.* "Let's call her Teresa," *she says.* "Do you think we could call her Teresa? I want to have some say about the name."

I walked to my grandmother's bed by the window on the left. I said: "In an hour you will be white and still. Where are you now?" *My grandmother was silent. She was dreaming of a vast expanse of snow. Where she dreamt, it was cold. But the air was clear. It was five o'clock on a February afternoon. She looked toward the horizon. I lay down on the cold floor next to my grandmother's bed. From where I lay, if I turned my head to the side, I could see Al in the far corner, in his coma.* "Al?" *I said. Al was sleeping.*

"This is the vestibule," *the voice said.* "You can't stay here."

"Where should I go?" *I asked.*

"Stay right where you are," *the voice said.* "In any case you have no choice. If I were you, I'd get some sleep."

"Then they'll be gone."

"They will," *the voice said.* "But the moon will rise. It can be counted on."

In the vestibule, on the floor beside my grandmother's bed, the snow began to fall.

*

"If pain is this twisting, or that chill, you must have company," Samuel said. "I will wash all the walls so they are clean."

Samuel, my lover, was talking to me from the ordinary world, the world of night and day, *where you are too.* I was surprised to see him among the dying. In the dim light his face was clearly visible. He looked at me thoughtfully.

"You can't stay here," I said. "You'll perish like the others."

"I will take you back with me," he said. "*Then*, I'll listen."

"Let's talk here. I want to stay with the dying. I love the *truth* around the dying," I said. "Let's stay in the room where they are dying, and where the snow falls soundlessly."

"Come back with me," Samuel said. "Tell me in the everyday world. *Al's* room is in there where *you* are and there the snow falls too thickly for me to hear you. Don't you see: the snow is gathering! Even your teacher, Isaac, cannot stay in this room."

I said, "Isaac is not my teacher. I don't have a teacher."

"But *if* you *had* one, if you were to look for one again, you could not look in there." Samuel and I stood face to face. I reached out to put my hand against his chest.

"You can't do that here," Samuel said. "Come back with me. You have listened to the stories that they want to tell. Now *I* want to tell one." I saw he wished to touch me, but he couldn't in this room. He looked at me. His eyes fixed on mine.

We sit across the table from each other in the room he has arranged for us to be in. The room is full of light.

"And Christa?"

"Christa's dead," Samuel said. "Those are the dead you're finished with."

"Oh, I don't think so."

"We must go back, Anna," he said again, deliberately. "Then you can look. We will look together."

"That isn't possible. You don't see what I see. You didn't see what I have seen."

"No," he agreed.

Snow was falling heavily in the darkness.

IV

.

"I'll go back with Samuel," I said to Isaac.

"Why?" Isaac, who needed no one, was curious.

"There's no difference between here and there. Also, Samuel sees me. I love Samuel."

"Sees you?" Isaac asked.

I looked up at Isaac. Isaac was sleeping. I opened my notebook anyway. I read to Isaac sleeping:

"I try to be impervious to the loud bee-sound that has been filling my left ear all day, to *all* the sounds—the wind, the sound of swallowing, the bird trilling. But I can't be impervious. The bee-sound drills through my head.

"Yesterday I went inside because the force of the blowing, streaming, green, glittering world outside is brutal. Beautiful, but brutal. It is raw, incorruptible, untransformable power. I went inside to be sheltered from the green, the blowing, the irreproachable force. But this morning I experience the same irreproachable, brutal force inside in the streaming and humming.

"I am unhoused, with no protection.

"The force is inescapable.

"I try to take a walk. But the light is too bright. There are too many distinct objects glittering and shining. All the shapes. The grains of sand on the side of the road glitter. So many objects. There are leaves rolled up, leaves unfurled. Leaves in all sizes and states of shine and unfolding are blown by the wind.

"The brightness, the gleaming, the bee-sound to the left of my ear, all flow into one stream and pour into my face.

"I am desolate. I am emptied out.

"The space around my head is cold, clear, empty, without qualities.

"Now the space (the force) arises from a slit made by a knife at the back of my left thigh, and the knife is drawn upward through the buttock and the whole body. I feel no pain. Horror. But not pain.

"There is sadness, beating, pulsing, tasting, a cool arising all *within* the substanceless space. But no boundary around each sensation.

"I can't find a self in this. No being is here.

"I am watching a relentless streaming. There's no relief. The streaming pulls everything into it. Out of it everything comes. There is just awareness and this vast streaming out of which pressure, moisture, heat, pulsing manifest themselves briefly. Feeling too. Sadness lasts one mind-moment. Then it disappears back into the undifferentiated, seamless streaming.

"This force is bright, hard, cold, immaculate. It is irreproachable. It isn't only violent. It is also pure, innocent, blameless.

"Do you hear me Isaac?" I looked up.

Isaac went on sleeping.

I said, "Nonetheless, I'll read you a bit more before I leave."

I read:

"At noon I walked outside. It is a perfect summer day. The sky is brilliant overhead. But light is draining out of the sky.

"Everything is moving, blowing, loud, serious, wonderful. But the wind with its ferocity is hollow. No substance to the wind, the day, the light.

"Everything before this moment has passed away.

"My body has been like a stone all day.

"There is the quick streaming across my face. The streaming is like wind, whipping my face to numbness. I am looking at awareness itself now.

"All the objects in awareness have dissolved.

"I am seeing my own dying. I am seeing the dying of each moment, moment after moment, at each moment perfect extinction. My body is nothing. My mind is nothing. Only dying is real.

"My head is wrapped in sweetness.

"The pouring is silent.

"I'm reading to you, Isaac."

*

Sr. Dassanīya walks on a country road. She is walking alone. The June green washes around her. It is midday and bright. The day is fully open. Her robes against her legs, the wind, thoughts come and go like gnats, meteors of aspiration, too fast beating of her heart. In Sr. Dassanīya's heart the question forms and dissolves: "What does the mind find beautiful?"

Wind blows against her face. Her gray eyes are clear. Her clear seeing is sweet.

Her practice is not for virtue, not for wisdom, not for serenity. Her practice is for the unshakable deliverance of the heart.

V

Samuel said: "You are talking about the dead."

"No," I said, "now I'm talking about the dying. But if you see the dead as real (Isaac does, and Al), you see how all your efforts not to be like them are futile."

"To be like the dying?"

"We *are* the dying," I said.

"But why spend time with them? Why go every day to work with them. Why choose work like that? The hospice is a house of death."

"And moreover," Samuel said. "Moreover," he continued. "Whom do you meet there? What do you do there?"

I grew impatient.

"What *do* you do?" Sam said. "With strangers." I see he fears the same hand that soothes the forehead of a dying man will then touch *him*.

We are lying on the kitchen floor. The cat circles around us, not without interest.

I feel Samuel's body as his will. There is cleaving, piercing, heat, a violent, widening force with no edge. This is another truth, gleaming and immaculate, that wells up in Samuel's body and in mine. We love to an opaline solitude. Damask.

Sam said, "With strangers?"

"Strangers are mysterious."

I met a man long ago who had lost his friends. He would find his friends or he would not find them.

"When I go into a room I haven't been in before, I don't know what kind of pain will be in there. But I go into the room. That's what I do.

"Sometimes the person is asleep. Unconscious. Or conscious, but absorbed in his pain. He feels the burning, the searing, beating, sharpness, twisting—. He is in the desert. He feels dharma in that heat. He sees that everything there is unalterable. He is somewhere he has never been, where I have been."

"And then?"

"Then," I said, "I try to pay attention. I stay in the awareness."

"Of what?" Sam said. He gets off the floor. I watch him put his trousers on. He stands over me.

"Of pain that is unfeatured. Pain before it has been scribbled over by all these stories.

"I attend to the voices. The voices are like bats in the daylight, like light on water under wind, like a rustling of snakes on desert sand, like the hum of bees":

I don't want to die. Only with great rending is the separation performed.

I want to die. *You who cleave to it are yet alive. I* will *die too, but not soon enough.*

Blessed are you who created pores, holes, orifices, channels, and ducts! If one should open or another close, it would be impossible to endure.

How long is it given to me to be in this world? Out of the depths I have called.

I beg you to stay by me for the rest of my day.

"The unconscious man is spectral. I listen to his breathing. His life speaks through his breathing. I breathe with him. His breath is my breath."

Of late my soul has been departing from me in the night, and not illuminating me with dreams, as was its wont.

Neither the sufferings nor their rewards are welcome to me.

"Then the voices thicken. My voices mingle with the cloud of voices. I hear my own voices for the first time."

She put a needle through my dog's heart

Red and yellow, silver and green are the colors of your treachery

I will break your bones. I will hold your mouth against a huge river

I do not know what pity is. And I never will know what pity is

When I am gone, who will behold the beauty? My name is Rachel.

Samuel shook his head.

I feel I should get up and cover myself, but I am compelled to remain naked, to appear in the light—to practice ruthless visibility. I turn away from Sam.

"One night I was at the hospice late. At night the hospice is another country. Everything is rude and twisted, lawful and unlawful. The hall lights are bright. I walked past a man's room. When he saw me I knew I must go in. I went in and saw a thin black man. He told me he was from Guyana where he harvests sugar cane."

"And he has cancer like the rest of them?" Sam asked.

"Like Al," I said. I sat up on the kitchen floor. I drew my knees against my chest. Samuel handed me my clothes. I laid them down next to me and continued:

"The man said, 'What did I do?'

"I thought: If I can't answer this question I've learned nothing. 'Pain doesn't come from action or inaction. Pain isn't anything you know, or I know. No one can free himself from pain. But suffering is a house you can unbuild. You have to keep the house whole enough so it doesn't fall in and crush you. With great care you must dismantle it piece by piece. I know this.'

"The hospice is blindingly bright, unsurvivable.

"I get into the bed with the man. I caress his forehead, the veins in the temple, very carefully his eyelids. I sing to him. My fingers follow the pulse from his throat to his chest on the left side. I feel the pulse of his life, of my life. They are the same and they are not the same. I feel his death. I feel my death that is real.

"On Monday, I went back to see the man. He accused me: 'Do you know what death means?' Thursday he told me: 'This world is a nest of gold and we are inside it.'"

"Oh, Anna." Samuel said my name as if he really knew it.

I am naked. Samuel, fully dressed, lies down beside me.

That night I dreamt of Margo. We are in the Guyanese man's hospice room. Al is also there. The winds come up, and little animals have made tracks in the sand, barely perceptible. Samuel can't be found anywhere. "The wind will kill you, but it is no matter," Al repeats himself. Margo begins to dream. I'm horrified. *I can see into her dream.* We are in the room with the dying animal. There is a lake in the room. Isaac is not there to help me. We hear the moaning of the animal. Margo says: "You never will be able to see it." Where has she learned cruelty? I try to turn away from her. Now all the sounds in the dream disappear. Mustard grows through the desert sand—for the valley is not a valley with woods and streams, but a desert. The sun is brilliant overhead. The sands shine and glitter. Only Margo and I are there, and the animal.

Sharon Cameron is William R. Kenan Professor of English
at The Johns Hopkins University. She is the author of nu-
merous books including *Choosing Not Choosing: Dickinson's
Fascicles* and *Thinking in Henry James.*

Library of Congress Cataloging-in-Publication Data
Cameron, Sharon.
 Beautiful work : a meditation on pain / Sharon
 Cameron.
 ISBN 0-8223-2508-X (cloth : alk. paper)
 1. Cameron, Sharon. 2. Spiritual biography—
United States. 3. Pain—Religious aspects—
Buddhism. 4. Literary historians—United States—
Biography. I. Title.
BQ944.M47 2000 818'.5403—dc21 [B] 99-059146